# SU-152/ISU-152
# VS
# TIGER

## Eastern Front 1943–45

## DAVID GREENTREE

OSPREY PUBLISHING
Bloomsbury Publishing Plc
Kemp House, Chawley Park, Cumnor Hill, Oxford OX2 9PH, UK
29 Earlsfort Terrace, Dublin 2, Ireland
1385 Broadway, 5th Floor, New York, NY 10018, USA
E-mail: info@ospreypublishing.com
www.ospreypublishing.com

OSPREY is a trademark of Osprey Publishing Ltd

First published in Great Britain in 2022

© Osprey Publishing Ltd, 2022

A catalogue record for this book is available from the British Library.

ISBN: PB 9781472848642; eBook 9781472848581;
ePDF 9781472848659; XML 9781472848598

22 23 24 25 26   10 9 8 7 6 5 4 3 2 1

Maps by Bounford.com
Colour artworks by Ian Palmer
Index by Rob Munro
Typeset by PDQ Digital Media Solutions, Bungay, UK
Printed and bound in India by Replika Press Private Ltd.

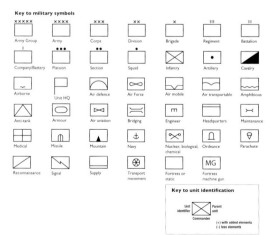

Front cover, above: An SU-152 moves forward. (Ian Palmer)
Front cover, below: A mid-production Tiger, with snow camouflage and
Zimmerit, advances along an Eastern Front road. (Ian Palmer)

Title page photo: ISU-152s of 343rd *TSAP*. (Courtesy of the Central Museum
of the Armed Forces, Moscow via Stavka)

Osprey Publishing supports the Woodland Trust, the UK's leading woodland
conservation charity.

To find out more about our authors and books visit
www.ospreypublishing.com. Here you will find extracts, author interviews,
details of forthcoming events and the option to sign up for our newsletter.

**A note on measure**
Both Imperial and metric measurements have been used in this book.
Conversion tables are provided below:
1in. = 2.54cm
1ft = 0.3m
1yd = 0.9m
1 mile = 1.6km
1lb = 0.45kg
1 long ton = 1.02 metric tonnes

1mm = 0.039in.
1cm= 0.39in.
1m = 1.09yd
1km = 0.62 miles
1kg = 2.2lb
1 metric tonne = 0.98 long tons

**Author's acknowledgements**
I would like to thank Major James Gebhardt (Ret'd) for his efforts spent
tirelessly translating Russian sources; without his assistance the book would be
lacking the opinions of the formation commanders as to the performance of
the SU-152/ISU-152. Combat descriptions would be missing a Soviet
perspective and the description of the engagement at Pleskau would not be
balanced. I would also like to show appreciation to my editor, Nikolai
Bogdanovic, for his patience and tolerance.

**Dedication**
This book is dedicated to Major James Gebhardt. Despite many setbacks, his
determination to keep on working was an inspiration to me. At 19 Jim was
enlisted and served with the US Army in Vietnam for three years. He gained a
commission whilst at Idaho University and graduated with an MA in History
from the University of Washington, Seattle. He commanded a squadron of
tanks in West Germany. He learnt Russian at Monterey, California, going on
to study at the US Army Russian Institute at Garmisch, West Germany. He
taught military history at the US Army Command and Staff College, and later
wrote the definitive history of the Petsamo-Kirkenes Operation. He retired
from active duty in 1992, and since then has spent his time translating
numerous memoirs and Soviet Naval Staff studies of the war.

# CONTENTS

# INTRODUCTION

Soviet concepts about the use of armoured forces in the 1930s envisaged large formations breaking through the enemy line and enveloping enemy formations. However, the purges of large swathes of senior officers in the late 1930s impeded the development of this doctrine. Instead, the use of armour as infantry support forces found popularity, hastened in late 1939 when large formations were temporarily dispensed with, following their combat deployment in Poland. The establishment once again of eight mechanized corps (MC) following the successful deployment of panzer divisions by Germany in France still meant 20 brigades of infantry support tanks were in existence. Only a few weeks prior to the invasion of the Soviet Union, the decision was taken to form these infantry support brigades into MC. The larger armoured formations could not compare to their German equivalents, because flexible command and control by experienced senior commanders, thus allowing junior officer initiative, was completely lacking. By July 1941, these large formations would be disbanded. In August new, small battalion-size brigades combining different types of tanks would be used.

The creation of larger formations began once again in the spring of 1942. Tank corps (TC) were comprised of a motorized rifle brigade (MRB) and three tank brigades (TB), with a combination of 138 heavy, medium and light tanks. Artillery was non-existent, except in the MRB's mortar and 76mm artillery battalions. The establishment of 13th MC with three mechanized brigades (MB), each comprising a tank regiment and three mechanized battalions, would begin in late 1942 to support the armour with infantry more effectively. The three tank regiments of the mechanized corps would be formed into a tank brigade in 1943, with some mechanized corps still operating tank regiments as well. The mechanized corps had a lot of guns (by early 1943, 36 45mm and 36 76mm guns) and some possessed about the same number of tanks as a tank

corps (204 light and medium in 1943 and 197 light and medium in 1944). A tank corps and a mechanized corps were certainly equal in strength to a panzer division in terms of armour, though in 1942 and early 1943 the Germans had better artillery support.

The use of heavy assault guns by Soviet formations originated in the lack of effective artillery support provided to armour by towed artillery. Indirect fire support weapons needed an extensive and flexible communications system and personnel capable of using it. Decentralized command and control, something of an anathema to the Soviet political system, was also required to best utilize the artillery's potential. Self-propelled guns on strongly armoured platforms could use direct fire and keep pace with the armour. From 10 January 1943 onward, each of the 25 tank corps was given one assault gun regiment and 36 120mm mortars. Initially, the assault gun regiment had 17 SU-76s and eight SU-122s, mounting 76mm and 122mm guns respectively. In May, this regiment was given SU-152s instead. In August, the towed anti-tank units belonging to TCs would be replaced with regiments of SU-76s and SU-85s. From August 1943, each mechanized corps would theoretically also have an SU-152 regiment, plus SU-76 and SU-85 units, though few corps would be equipped with a full complement of SP guns until 1945. The creation of tank armies (TA) began in late 1942, consisting

A Tiger from *Das Reich* at Kursk. During the Kursk battle two Tiger battalions would be used, one on each flank of the Kursk salient. There would also be four companies of Tigers belonging to Panzergrenadier Division *Grossdeutschland* (PGD *GD*) and three SS PDs on the southern side. The Soviets, aware of the Tiger's potency, organized heavy armoured battalions and self-propelled gun (SPG) regiments to counter them. Because limited numbers of the SPG would be available, T-34s would be ordered to close with the Tigers rapidly and target their side armour. (ullstein bild/ullstein bild via Getty Images)

The mounting of the ML-20 Model 37 152mm gun on the chassis of a KV tank to form the SU-152 was the most notable SPG development, due to the large calibre of the gun. It was not only the armour formations that would use heavy assault guns. Infantry armies with organic or attached tank brigades or independent tank regiments could be supported by SP guns. Assault guns of various calibres would be attached to attacking infantry units, especially assault battalions, to break through enemy fortified positions and counter the appearance of German armoured forces. (Courtesy of the Central Museum of the Armed Forces, Moscow via Stavka)

**OPPOSITE**
The Eastern Front, 1943–45

usually of one mechanized corps plus two tank corps supported by a light artillery brigade (with towed 76mm guns). These changes addressed the lack of high-explosive capability within the tank corps to attack German infantry and gun positions.

The German leadership soon experienced the technological superiority of Soviet armour. In 1942, German designers were given six months to produce the Tiger, a symbol of German technological superiority, to combat the KV-1 and T-34. Once operational, the Tiger's ability to withstand enemy anti-tank (AT) rounds hitting its armour justified to German commanders the immense cost of producing them. The Tiger was vitally important to the German leadership's strategic decisions that would be taken on the basis of what it thought could be achieved by the system. The Soviet winter offensive in 1942/43 and the German spring counter-offensive had created a 90-mile salient around Kursk, splitting two German army groups. This bulge would be the target of a pincer movement. The offensive was postponed until sufficient numbers of heavy German armour could be brought to the front, giving the Soviets time to fortify along the lines of approach. Instead of attacking the weakest part of the line with the Tiger and other heavy armour such as the Panther, German commanders were convinced they could bludgeon through a heavily defended enemy line. Following the blunting of the German panzer force at Kursk in July 1943, Soviet tank armies would launch successful summer campaigns, shattering the myth of German armoured superiority. The strategic initiative would decisively pass to the Soviets.

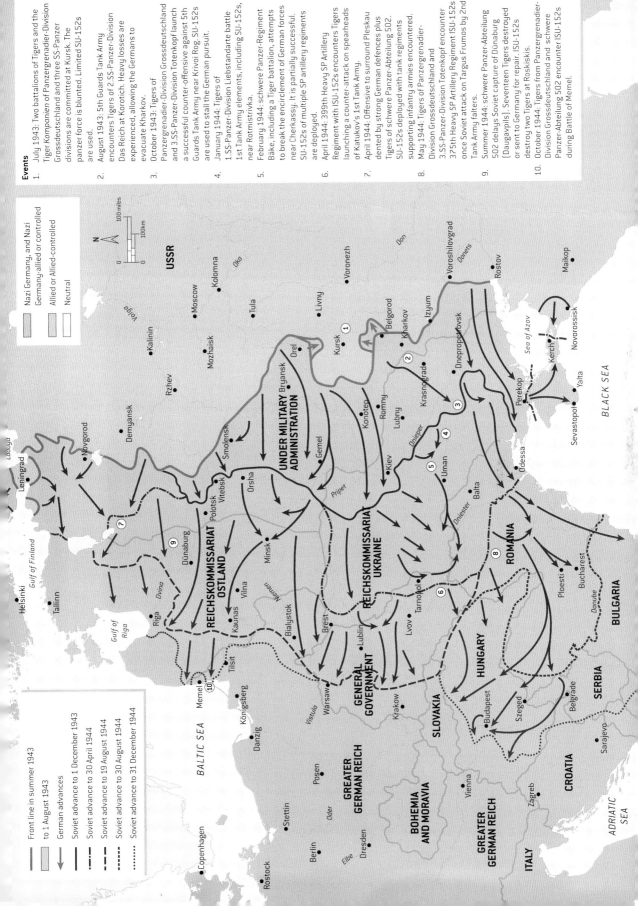

## Events

1. July 1943: Two battalions of Tigers and the Tiger *Kompanien* of Panzergrenadier-Division Grossdeutschland and three SS-Panzer divisions are committed at Kursk. The panzer force is blunted. Limited SU-152s are used.

2. August 1943: 5th Guards Tank Army encounters Tigers of 2.SS-Panzer-Division Das Reich at Korotich. Heavy losses are experienced, allowing the Germans to evacuate Kharkov.

3. October 1943: Tigers of Panzergrenadier-Division Grossdeutschland and 3.SS-Panzer-Division Totenkopf launch a successful counter-offensive against 5th Guards Tank Army near Krivoi Rog. SU-152s are used to stall the German pursuit.

4. January 1944: Tigers of 1.SS-Panzer-Division Liebstandarte battle 1st Tank Army elements, including SU-152s, near Rotmistrivka.

5. February 1944: schwere Panzer-Regiment Bäke, including a Tiger battalion, attempts to break the encirclement of German forces near Cherkassy. It is partially successful. SU-152s of multiple SP artillery regiments are deployed.

6. April 1944: 399th Heavy SP Artillery Regiment with ISU-152s encounters Tigers launching a counter-attack on spearheads of Katukov's 1st Tank Army.

7. April 1944: Offensive to surround Pleskau dented by strong German defences plus Tigers of schwere Panzer-Abteilung 502. SU-152s deployed with tank regiments supporting infantry armies encountered.

8. May 1944: Tigers of Panzergrenadier-Division Grossdeutschland and 3.SS-Panzer-Division Totenkopf encounter 375th Heavy SP Artillery Regiment ISU-152s once Soviet attack on Targus Frumos by 2nd Tank Army falters.

9. Summer 1944: schwere Panzer-Abteilung 502 delays Soviet capture of Dünaburg (Daugavpils). Seventeen Tigers destroyed or sent to Germany for repair. ISU-152s destroy two Tigers at Roskiskis.

10. October 1944: Tigers from Panzergrenadier-Division Grossdeutschland and schwere Panzer-Abteilung 502 encounter ISU-152s during Battle of Memel.

### Legend

- Front line in summer 1943
- to 1 August 1943
- German advances
- Soviet advance to 1 December 1943
- Soviet advance to 30 April 1944
- Soviet advance to 19 August 1944
- Soviet advance to 30 August 1944
- Soviet advance to 31 December 1944

- Nazi Germany, and Nazi Germany-allied or controlled
- Allied or Allied-controlled
- Neutral

# CHRONOLOGY

## 1942

**April**
Porsche and Henschel produce prototype tanks mounting an 8.8cm gun. Henschel is chosen to start mass production.
The KV-3 chassis designed to mount a 152mm gun is discontinued and the KV-7 chassis is approved in its place.

**September**
First combat deployment of the Tigers of 502nd Heavy Panzer Battalion to the Eastern Front near Lake Ladoga. The battalion has a complement of Panzer (Pz) IIIs supporting its Tigers.

**December**
The Main Artillery Directorate (*GAU*) orders the ZIK-20 (KV-14) design to replace the KV-7 as the chassis to mount the 152mm gun.

## 1943

**January**
Two additional Tiger battalions are established to complement the three already operational.
The KV-14 is tested at Chelyabinsk.

**February**
The first 30 SU-152s (KV-14) are produced. Some 670 will be completed by January 1944.

**March**
New organization for the Tiger battalions dispenses with the Pz IIIs and mandates full strength of 45 Tigers.
Initial 16 SU-152 regiments formed, designated as a self-propelled artillery regiment (*SAP*) of six batteries each of two SU-152s.

**July**
The German panzer forces are blunted at Kursk. Tigers of two battalions plus Tiger companies of Panzergrenadier Division *Grossdeutschland* (PGD *GD*) and three *SS* Panzer Divisions are committed, though to limited effect. Only a small number of SU-152s are used.

**August**
Tigers survive Kursk unscathed and help delay the Soviet pursuit during the subsequent Belgorod–Kharkov operation.

**October**
PGD *GD* and *SS* Panzer Division *Totenkopf* launch counter-offensive at Krivoi Rog.
ISU-152 prototype based on IS-1 tested.

**December**
Forty-six ISU-152s produced. On average, 100 will be produced per month, for a total of 1,885 by May 1945.

## 1944

**February**
Heavy Panzer Regiment Bäke with a Tiger battalion attempts to break the Soviet encirclement near Cherkassy.

**March**
*SAP* units begin to be taken out of the line, to be re-equipped with ISU-152s. They are given Guards status and named heavy self-propelled artillery regiments (*TSAP*).

| | | | |
|---|---|---|---|
| **April** | 1st Guards Tank Army (GTA), commanded by General Mikhail Katukov, reaches Bukovina. Tigers of 506th Heavy Panzer Battalion encounter ISU-152s of 399th *TSAP*. Pleskau offensive to the south of Lake Peipus fails to break German infantry positions supported by 502nd Heavy Panzer Battalion elements. Tigers encounter 33rd Guards Heavy Tank Regiment (GHTR) with SU-152s. | **July** | Tigers of 502nd Heavy Panzer Battalion defends the approaches to Dünaburg (Daugavpils). Equipping of other Tiger battalions with King Tigers begins. |
| **May** | Tigers of PGD *GD* and *Totenkopf* defeat Soviet advance by 2nd Guards Tank Army on Targus Frumos. | **October** | Tigers of 502nd Heavy Panzer Battalion and PGD *GD* defend Memel. |
| **June** | Operation *Bagration* launched. *TSAP* extensively employed with tank and infantry armies. | **1945** **January** | Soviet offensive advances through eastern Germany. Some Tiger battalions still use Tigers; most are equipped with King Tigers. |
| | | **March** | ISU-152s effectively deploy to urban environments like Breslau. |

Although losses at Kursk in 1943 were on the whole recoverable, the might of the German armour had failed; the Soviet defensive line, built in the spring with a firm conviction the Germans would attack, proved too strong. The German command traditionally attacked where defences were the weakest and would seek to encircle the strongest part of the enemy line; instead, at Kursk it went for the strongest part of the line and would fight a battle of attrition. The Red Army would win because the Soviets' industrial capacity was superior to that of the Germans. They needed to build quickly, as the commitment of 5th Guards Tank Army to halt the SS Panzers at Prokhorovka would prove to be expensive. T-34 crews mistook the Pz IV with *schuerzen* (skirt armour) for Tigers, and thought they needed to close the range to knock them out. Pz IV crews could pick them off as they approached. (Photo by Heinrich Hoffmann/ullstein bild via Getty Images)

# DESIGN AND DEVELOPMENT

## SOVIET

The idea for producing the SU-152 originated in the need to destroy concrete bunkers encountered in the war with Finland. Earlier prototypes existed in the 1930s; however, the developers of these systems were arrested in the purges. Those designed in late 1939 were deployed in small numbers only and similarly discontinued. In August 1940, Major General Sergey Shevchenko, the deputy chief of the Main Artillery Directorate (*GAU*), signed off on the design requirement for a self-propelled 152mm gun. A prototype was ordered for 1 December based on the KV chassis. The *GAU* Artillery Committee received a letter from the Kirov Factory signed by T.N. Golburt, the system's chief designer, regarding issues with the design of the SP gun, stating the KV chassis was too heavy to match the weight limit the *GAU* stipulated. While the *GAU* was responsible for the gun, the Main Automotive Armoured Tank Directorate (*GABTU*) was in charge of the chassis. The SP gun had to be loaded onto a railcar and needed to weigh less than 60 tons. The Kirov Factory thought the prototype would be 65 tons. The *GAU* suggested the turret armour thickness could be reduced. The first hull was received at the Kirov Factory in March 1941; however, other work had higher priority following reports on German armour design, including work on the heavy armour of the KV-1 and KV-2. By 27 May, the requirement had changed; the Central Committee of the Communist Party stated a 152mm BR-2 gun based on an elongated KV chassis (KV-3, termed

Project 212) was needed to destroy bunkers, with ten units to be built by the end of the year. Also, Marshal G.I. Kulik, former chief of the *GAU* (1935–39, and from 1939 Deputy People's Commissar of Defence), said that in order to destroy enemy armour a naval B-13 130mm gun and new 107mm AT gun would have SP mounts; prototypes were ordered for 1 September and 1 October, respectively, on the same chassis as the 152mm BR-2 prototype.

When Germany invaded, Project 212 was sent to the Ural Heavy Machinery Plant (*UZTM*) in Sverdlovsk, where KV-1 hulls for the Chelyabinsk Tractor Factory were made, and where the M-30 122mm howitzer was being constructed. The factories building the KVs were moved to Chelyabinsk. The disturbance hindered rapid progress with Project 212. In November, the *GAU* stipulated that the work schedule in 1942 should include work on the project and 85mm and 76mm SP guns. In the spring of 1942, the KV-3 chassis was discontinued as the base for the 152mm SP gun. Instead, the KV assault gun prototype, named KV-7, with a 76mm and two 45mm guns in the turret, would be used because the assault gun project would soon be discontinued. The triple gun system was too difficult; however, the large superstructure of the KV-7 was suitable to mount heavy howitzers. The State Defence Committee (*GKO*) stipulated the 152mm gun would be placed on the KV-7 chassis. Project 212 and the KV-3 were shut down by the spring of 1942 and the Chelyabinsk Factory had no plans to revive them.

By the summer of 1943, each tank corps (TC) had a motorized rifle brigade (MRB) and three tank brigades (TB) (162 light and medium tanks). In late 1943, light tanks were dispensed with and the TB was based on three battalions, each with two companies of ten T-34s. The TB's motorized infantry battalion was made into a sub-machine gun (SMG) battalion. The TC (70 light tanks and 98 T-34s in 1943, and 208 T-34s in 1944), lacking infantry and gun support, could not hold the ground gained. (Sovfoto/Universal Images Group via Getty Images)

On 15 April, the *GAU* Artillery Committee approved the KV-7 and ML-20 Model 37 152mm gun combination. The conceptual design was finished on 4 August and officially proposed on 3 September. The Kirov Factory had several hulls with turrets already made. The barrel and breech could be taken from the ML-20; however, the cradle and recoil mechanism had to be redesigned to have a shorter recoil length in order to fit the ML-20 system into the existing KV-7 turret (termed U-18), a solution which helped with the turret weight and height.

There was a competitor to the U-18 created by F.F. Petrov at the People's Commissariat of Arms Factory No. 8, who also worked at the *UZTM* building, designated the ZIK-20. He wanted to modify the ML-20 gun in order to give equal priority to both indirect and direct fire. The result was to make the gun too high to fit in the existing KV-7 design. The *GAU* Artillery Committee had other reservations as well. The turret sides were less sloped than the U-18; the gun was located further forward, increasing pressure on the front road wheels; shells were stowed on racks on the sides of the superstructure, increasing the threat of an explosion if hit; and fuel cells on the sides of the vehicle also increased the risk of an explosion.

The Soviet military leadership decided to hurry things along. The inability of towed artillery to manoeuvre in deep snow hastened the need for SP guns. A special team was put together at the Chelyabinsk Tractor Factory to work on the project, with L.S. Troyanov in charge. Designers from *UZTM* helped. The design of J.Y. Kotin, the chief designer at the Chelyabinsk Tractor Factory, was implemented because he made the least changes. A prototype, designated the KV-14, was completed by the end of 1942. Both this project and the others would be displayed on 3 January 1943 to the Main Artillery Directorate. Petrov's ML-20 would be used on the KV-1S chassis, with the prototype to be tested on 31 January near Chelyabinsk. The stipulations to the designers were: combat weight not to exceed 45.5 tonnes, 20 rounds carried, armour thickness of the fighting compartment 60mm, frontal armour of the fighting compartment 60–75mm, the height of the fighting compartment 170cm, and the rate of fire 3–4 rounds per minute.

The *GAU* stated the role of the 152mm SP gun would be to destroy bunkers, earth and timber emplacements, and other strong field fortifications by direct fire from close range in operations breaking through enemy defences, and for combating enemy guns and defences further back. Angles of fire in elevation would be from minus three to plus 20 degrees and traverse six degrees to each side. Sights were needed to support both direct fire from unconcealed positions and indirect fire from cover. The position of the traversing mechanism flywheel relative to the panoramic sight eyepiece and the gunner's seat had to permit the gunner to keep his eye on the eyepiece. A 9-R radio was to be installed for external communication. The commander was to have a PTK panoramic sight and the gunner an ST-10 telescopic sight. At first the T-9 sight from the KV-2 was used, as it was available because production of the KV-2 had stopped.

Factory 200 installed the superstructure plates on the KV-1S hull. Factory 172 produced the SP version of the ML-20. The system was mounted on a frame with armoured protection and a large mantlet. The experience in making the KV-7 was integral to the completion of the KV-14. Side plates were angled to increase the probability of ricochet, even though the interior space was reduced. Five vision blocks were installed, though they were not located right at the edge of the superstructure

# SU-152

From October 1943, the SU-152 would be produced with exhaust fans. SU-152s would not routinely be painted with any camouflage except in winter when whitewash could be applied. Production in meaningful quantities ceased by the end of 1943, because the German long-barrelled 75mm on the Pz IV was capable of knocking out the SP gun from the front from 1,000m.

The decision was made in late 1942 to take the KV heavy tanks out of the tank battalion. The KV-1Ss were instead formed into GHTRs with four companies of four KVs each. The lighter KV-1S was quicker compared to the KV model 1942, though its armour was thinner. Some 1,300 would be built. A sub-machine gun (SMG) company and pioneer platoon would be added in February 1944. Sometimes SU-152s would join these formations to replace losses. KV-1S production ceased by the late summer of 1943. Some KV-85s mounting an 85mm gun in a new turret atop the KV-1S chassis (as pictured above) would then be built. (From the fonds of the *RGAKFD* in Krasnogorsk via Stavka)

roof, leaving some blind zones around the vehicle. The KV-14 was supposed to have a crew of six; however, the fighting compartment had no room for a radio operator and instead the radio was placed in front of the commander's position. The standard fuel tanks of the KV-1 could not be used and instead fuel cells with a capacity of 480 litres were placed on the sides of the superstructure. Designers had difficulty in finding a place for the ammunition. The main rack was on the left side of the superstructure, with a second group located under the gun, difficult for the crew to access. The fighting compartment was spacious, with the crew being able to stand without bending; the commander, loader and gunner had folding seats. Rather than an SP gun to destroy fortifications, the KV-14 was a general-purpose assault gun.

The Kirov Factory was ordered to produce 30 guns in February and 75 in March, and 35 hulls in February and 100 in March. Delays caused only 15 completed SU-152s to be produced in February. The Kirov Plant was producing the KV-1S plus the T-34. The schedule was ambitiously increased to 90 completed SU-152s in March to correct the deficit. This was achieved only in the last three days; only 28 were completed by 28 March. Production defects started to show in 36 vehicles when the SU-152 arrived with the units in April. This delayed the combat debut until July. Issues with component supplies delayed production in April and May. While the target of 75 was achieved in April, only 25 of 75 were completed the following month. The quota of 80 SU-152s was met in July.

This occurred when the Tiger was operating at the front. When tests were performed on a Tiger captured intact, designers had to work out the best way to combat them. The BR-540 AP round was developed for the SU-152 in the summer of 1943 and issued to the units in August. Issues with poor workmanship to the storage racks were identified, meaning only four instead of six shells could be placed in them. When crews increased the basic load to 25 rounds, the additional five rounds

# ISU-152 COMPARTMENT

1. 152mm gun
2. Panoramic sight
3. Telescopic sight
4. Propellant casings
5. Gunner's seat
6. Shells with charges in shelf storage
7. Shells with charges in clamp storage
8. Rammer
9. Commander's seat
10. Loader's seat

lay beneath the gun, the shells and cases on the floor, held in place by blocks. The additional rack proposed was never made. In September, 109 SU-152s were manufactured. Some of the last vehicles produced in September had fans in their roofs, added when a crewman commented exhaust gases were entering the fighting compartment. Four SU-152s were produced in December and the last two in January. A total of 670 SU-152s would be manufactured. The Kirov Factory was by then busy producing the ISU-152.

On 25 May 1943, Factory 100 was ordered to modernize the SU-152 to include better armour protection. In July, Kotin supervised the project with G.N. Moskvin as the main designer. The need for thicker frontal armour was identified. The ISU-152 based on the IS-1 chassis was slightly longer, higher and heavier, though slightly narrower compared to the SU-152. The ISU-152 would use the same gun as the SU-152. The ISU-152 side plates had less incline (75 degrees) and the fighting compartment was slightly larger. To compensate for the loss of incline, the side plates were made thicker, from 75mm to 90mm. The initial prototype was successfully tested in October 1943. The crew found the fighting compartment was better designed compared to that of the SU-152. Some 303 shots were fired; the gun was found to be as effective as the towed 152mm gun. Firing while mobile did not work, but firing while at a brief halt was effective. Aimed rate of fire was 2–2.5 rounds per minute. Some issues did surface. The mounting of the panoramic sight had to be redone. The gunner's seat was not positioned conveniently; a proposal was made to make it folding and lower. The gun on the first ISU-152s produced could only be elevated by 18 degrees instead of the mandated 20 degrees. When turning sideways by seven degrees, the panoramic sight rested on the edge of the hatch.

In December, the SU-152 and ISU-152 were both produced at Chelyabinsk, with 46 ISU-152s made. In January 1944, 50 ISU-152s would be produced, 75 the following month, 150 in March and 130 in April. On average, 100 would be produced every month from then on. Defects found in January were much less common and, instead of 72 hours spent on assembly, they would be completed in 24 to 30 hours. Some 1,885 would be produced from December 1943 to May 1945. By the end of February 1945, the frontal part of the ISU-152 was welded, making it more durable.

The decision to mount the A-19S 122mm gun on the ISU chassis with 30-round stowage capacity was made in 1943. The prototype was built at Chelyabinsk in December. The State Defence Committee adopted the ISU-122 for service in March 1944 and the first vehicles would be completed in April. The A-19S gun rate of fire was low (1.5 shots per minute) because the breech had to be operated manually. The D-25 122mm gun, installed on the IS-2, was a semi-automatic variant and in September 1944 was fitted on the ISU-122. Rate of fire increased to 2–3 shots per minute (four if two loaders sat in the fighting compartment) and the crew benefited from shorter recoil, and 30 rounds could be carried. The ST-18 telescopic sight was calibrated for ranges out to 1.5km. The ISU-122 was a dedicated tank destroyer. Some 1,335 ISU-122s would be built from April 1944 to April 1945. Sometimes ISU-152s and ISU-122s would be in the same regiment at the same time, though this was thought to be avoided, because supply issues providing two types of ammunition resulted. The guns had different ballistics, too, and this doubled the effort when working out firing solutions.

# ISU-152

The ISU-152 started to be issued to self-propelled artillery units (SAPs) from the late winter of 1943/44. When this occurred, the regiment would be brought out of the line, provided with additional crews, assigned further training and be given Guards status. Thicker frontal and side armour compensated for the reduction of the slant angle, implemented in order to enlarge the fighting compartment. This made for better working conditions for the crew. The Pz IV would not be able to knock out the ISU-152 from the front.

The SU-152 could be used to fire bombardments prior to the assault; however, issues with reloading persuaded commanders to use towed artillery if available. The 152mm ML-20 Model 37 (shown here) was designed by F.F. Petrov, and was used to equip artillery regiments belonging to infantry armies. The ML-20 was also issued to artillery regiments of the reserve. The gun targeted enemy artillery positions to 17.23km. The German equivalent, the 15cm *schwere Feldhaubitze* (heavy field cannon) *sFH* 18, had a 13.3km range. A tractor could tow the gun, though these were in short supply. Armoured formations frequently did not have towed guns to support them, because they did not have the mobility to accompany the armour once they had broken through the enemy lines. Conversely, the SU-152 could rapidly advance to support the armour. (Courtesy of the Central Museum of the Armed Forces, Moscow via Stavka)

The 152mm ML-20S was supposed to be replaced with the 152mm BL-8 or BL-10 from May 1944. The BL-8 gun was a high-powered version designed to combat heavily armoured German SP guns. This longer 50cal gun could fire an HE round weighing 43.56kg at 880m/s. The AP round, weighing 48.78kg, could be fired at 850m/s. The round could penetrate 203mm of armour set at 90 degrees at ranges of 2,000m. In trials in July, it was discovered that the crew found the gun difficult to operate, and the muzzle brake and breech block were unreliable. The gun protruding a long way from the hull limited manoeuvrability. In August, the BL-8 was replaced with the shorter 48.5cal BL-10 gun. The vehicle was designated ISU-152-2. In December, trials showed issues with the barrel strength and the needed changes could not be done prior to the end of the war.

# GERMAN

In the 18th century, the Prussian Army, by operating on interior lines of communication, decisively defeated multiple numerically superior enemies through bold offensives, causing opponents severe losses and weakening the enemy's political willingness to fight. German military doctrine since the 1850s was still dominated by the cult of the offensive. The use of superior technology in a few short bold engagements had succeeded in the Wars of Unification; in World War I, the Schlieffen Plan in 1914 tried to knock France out of the war in a month prior to Russia fully mobilizing. Clausewitz suggested in the early 19th century that decisive engagements by armies with a moral and physical superiority won wars; defensive operations would only be necessary to build sufficient offensive power. Many German commanders misunderstood him and thought tactical offensive engagements would be sufficient to fight a successful defensive campaign, despite numerical weaknesses. The 1918 offensive on the Western Front was a good example of a weakened army trying to defeat Britain and France prior to full US mobilization. Though initially achieved, gains could not be exploited because of a lack of supplies and reinforcements, and the cost of the offensive would bring about the defeat of the German Army within eight months. German military commanders did not see this strategy as discredited; instead they blamed politicians on the home front for stabbing them in the back and signing the Versailles Peace Treaty.

The panzer arm developed in the 1930s was a less costly way of breaking through enemy lines. Germany, constrained in World War I from building an empire on other continents, would seek to expand eastward in the next war by occupying vast tracts of the Soviet Union. This could be done by large, fast-moving panzer forces operating as independent formations with mobile infantry and engineer elements, supported by *Luftwaffe* aircraft flying close air support missions. Leaders were taught to take the initiative, plan the attack and carry it out ruthlessly. Tactical victories would lead to strategic success by breaking the enemy's physical and moral strength. Identifying the weakest point in the enemy's defences and hitting it with the best weapons operated by the best-trained personnel to break through and envelop his armies would shatter the enemy. Heavy armour would target AT positions with smoke or high-explosive; alternatively, the enemy's AT guns could be suppressed by artillery or MGs. When the line broke, enemy armour would counter-attack. The primary aim of the long-range and heavier guns of heavy armour would be to deal with this counter-attack. The medium panzers could then exploit and Panzergrenadiers could eliminate pockets of

The invasion of the Soviet Union, Operation *Barbarossa*, showed the technological inferiority of German armour compared to the T-34 and KV-1. As many German armoured vehicles were being lost as could be built, despite the immense geographical gains achieved. In contrast, by 1942, the Red Army had created 100-plus independent tank battalions for the support of infantry; this declined to 28 by the end of 1943. In September 1942, separate tank regiments would replace them; by January 1943 they comprised a small light company and three T-34 companies with an SMG company. The 502nd Heavy Tiger Battalion would first encounter the KV-1 (shown here) when deployed to Army Group North in the winter of 1942/43. Though the armour was good and on the 1942 model practically safe from a hit from a Pz III or IV on the front slope, the gun could not easily defeat the Tiger's armour. (Sovfoto/Universal Images Group via Getty Images)

enemy resistance. Battles in France would be won by the use of mediocre panzers operated by personnel who had the better training, not by superior technology. The vehicle used in the heavy armour role was the Pz IV equipped with the short-barrelled 7.5cm gun.

German military leaders faced with the challenge of the size and technical proficiency of the Red Army sought the annihilation of the enemy and thought they had the weapon to achieve this with the Tiger. Two firms produced prototypes in 1942: Porsche and Henschel. Krupp was told to produce a turret for a modification of the 8.8cm *KwK* 36 L/56 for the Porsche design, while Rheinmetall produced a turret and high-velocity 75mm AT gun for the Henschel design. The 75mm gun project was stopped, as it needed specialized materials not available in sufficient quantities for a mass-produced weapon. Instead, the Krupp weapon would be installed on the Henschel prototype, capable of penetrating 100mm of armour at 1,000m using a *Panzergranate* 39 (*Pzgr* 39) shell. Porsche's prototype was favoured when Hitler inspected both on 20 April 1942. The connection of the transmission to two engines by Porsche was a mechanical problem and the Porsche prototype was beaten by the Henschel prototype in trials in the summer. Henschel could produce all the components and promised quicker production. The Porsche hull would be the Ferdinand SP gun, mounting the long-barrelled 8.8cm gun. Thirty-four Tigers would be produced per month in the first few months.

The Army General Staff realized not enough Tigers could be produced to allocate one Tiger company per panzer battalion. The decision to concentrate them into

# TIGER, 3RD SS PANZER DIVISION

Shown here is a Tiger belonging to the 9th Coy of Pz Regt 3 of the SS Panzer Division *Totenkopf,* , in the late summer of 1943. The Tiger has the old commander's cupola, rubber road wheels and two headlights on the front hull. These Tigers also had the older engine. By September, five Tigers with new commander's cupolas would arrive. Being the last company in the battalion, the three-digit identification number on the turret starts with a nine. The company had four platoons of five Tigers in the late summer of 1943. This tank is from the third platoon in the ninth company, and is tank no. 3, as indicated by the two digits after the nine on the turret.

The Tiger would soon begin to show its dominance of the battlefield when conditions permitted. Commanders thought better technology was needed to fight numerous, smaller engagements. The importance of superior technology also satisfied notions of racial superiority. (Nik Cornish at www.Stavka.org.uk)

independent heavy battalions was made; dispersing Tigers in penny packets to support other panzer units was not thought to be a good idea because maintenance resources needed to be centralized. The first three battalions would be created in May 1942. On the Tiger's first deployment a platoon of four got stuck in the mud near Lake Ladoga in September 1942. Then enemy rounds hit, destroying the barrel of one, immobilizing another. The engine of a third caught fire, creating a burning wreck the Soviets then captured.

Despite the questioning of the Tiger programme, and the fact that factories could produce double the number of Pz IVs, the German leadership demanded an expansion of production. Self-propelled guns would be produced in larger numbers from late 1943 to function as defensive weapons, as they were cheaper alternatives, despite the persistent belief in the Tiger as the epitome of the offensive spirit of the German Army. Production costs of Tigers were high, and despite the expansion of production in 1943, only 1,348 would be built. Instead of being satisfied with the Tiger, Hitler would order a heavier version to be developed. Reports of maintenance and supply issues would be ignored.

# TIGER, 507TH HEAVY PANZER BATTALION

This is a Tiger belonging to 507th Heavy Panzer Battalion, in the summer of 1944 with the battalion's camouflage pattern. The turret has tracks on the turret for added protection, Zimmerit paste, a single headlight and a low profile commander's cupola. The numbering system for the battalion was quite peculiar with a full-size first numeral and two others at about 60 per cent size. Tigers would soon have tracks on the whole side of the turret with identification numbers painted on them.

# TECHNICAL SPECIFICATIONS

## SOVIET

The crew, gun and shells of the SU-152 were in the front of the armoured fighting compartment, constructed from armour plates with a thickness of 20mm, 30mm, 60mm and 75mm. Three crew members were to the left of the gun, two to the right. Armour thickness on the upper and lower hull side, lower hull front, superstructure front and gun mantlet was 60mm. Upper front armour was 75mm. Armour plates above the engine and fighting compartment roof could be taken off. A large number of holes and hatches existed in the hull, for example for loading ammunition, firing personal weapons, viewing the outside, installing torsion bars and draining oil and fuel. On the roof of the engine compartment was a large hatch, with an opening for pouring water into the cooling system. The crew used a single hatch and double hatch on the roof. A round hatch to the left of the gun was for the extension to the panoramic sight and could be used by the crew in an emergency. Another escape hatch was located on the floor at the front. The hatches to enter and exit had three periscopes for observing the outside environment from within the vehicle.

The ISU-152 had different versions depending on the hull used (IS-1, IS-2 or IS-2 Model 1944). The early versions had three hatches in the roof and an emergency hatch on the floor of the hull with armoured cover. Later types had a fourth round hatch on the roof on the right. Armour protection was much improved from the SU-152, with

# SOVIET ST-10 GUNSIGHT

The ST-10 sight was calibrated for a range to 900m. A second panoramic sight was used for targets at greater ranges. Issues with switching between the sights meant batteries of guns would often concentrate on single targets in order to guarantee a hit through the number of shells fired rather than accuracy. The panoramic sight had a special extension cable for viewing through the left round hatch in the roof.

The ST-10 had a magnification of × 2 plus 18 degrees field of view. The left scale was for the OF-540 HE fragmentation plus the BR-540 AP round. The crew used a table to convert from HE, as the shells had different velocities. For example, 3,240m for the OF-540 shell was the same as 3,000m for the AP shell. Increments were in 100m up to 5,800m. The second and third scales were for the reduced and full charge OF-530 anti-concrete shell.

75mm on the upper hull side, 90mm on the lower hull front, lower hull side and superstructure front, and 100mm on the mantlet (increased to 120mm on the IS-2 model). The IS-2 model had larger capacity fuel tanks.

The ML-20, offset to the right and installed in a gimbal-type mount, had an elevation of from minus five to plus 18 degrees on the SU-152 and minus three to plus 20 degrees on the ISU-152. Both the elevation and deflection hand wheels were on the left of the barrel rather than one on each side, as on the towed ML-20. With a barrel length of 29cal, the direct fire range was 3,800m and the long range for indirect fire was 6,200m. A shell could be fired out to 800–900m with a flat trajectory. An electric trigger was used, though a manual mechanism could be used if this failed.

In early January 1943, the SU-152 prototype travelled 85km to a test range on a road covered in snow at an outside temperature of minus 42 degrees Celsius. The engine stalled frequently and the journey took 13 hours. Some 234 rounds were fired, averaging 2.8 rounds per minute using the first rack of shells (the *GAU* committee specified 3–4 rounds per minute were needed for the operational environment), with no warping in the gun or the mounting parts. Depending on the rack used, reloading took up to 30 seconds. The SP gun recoiled 70mm to 250mm once fired and the vehicle's stern fell by between 10mm and 80mm. Five rounds were fired at ranges of 200m, 400m, 600m and 800m after halting for a short time. The accuracy of the rounds was found to be acceptable, especially for a gun targeting fortifications. The 88km return route was covered in 6.8 hours, as the temperature had increased to minus 16 degrees Celsius. The operating speed was 13km/hr and the cruising speed 20km/hr.

# SOVIET AMMUNITION

The BR-540 AP projectile (**1**), weighing 48.8kg and with a muzzle velocity of 600m/s, could penetrate 105mm, 95mm, 85mm and 75mm of armour when fired at armour sloped at 60 degrees from ranges of 500m, 1,000m, 1,500m and 2,000m, respectively. This increased to 125mm, 115mm, 105mm and 90mm when fired at armour sloped at 90 degrees.

The BR-540B round, with ballistic cap, is shown at (**2**). A version was brought into service early in 1945 with slightly better capability at the longer ranges and did not bounce off sloped armour to the same degree. The 20 shells and propellant charges were stored on the walls of the fighting compartment. The typical load of shells was 13 HE and seven AP or concrete piercing.

The BR-540 was base detonated by an MD-7 fuse. The two silver-coloured bands had a slightly larger diameter compared to the projectile and served to centre the shell in the barrel. The copper-coloured bands expanded upon contact with the propellant charge to make a tight seal and push the projectile out of the barrel.

The 152mm OF-540 HE fragmentation projectile (**3**), with muzzle velocity of 606m/s at full charge, weighed 43.56kg and had 6kg of TNT. The G-545 concrete-piercing shell with OF-530 HE fragmentation projectile (**4**) had a muzzle velocity of 615m/s. The latter was base detonated, whereas the OF-540 had its detonator at the top of the round.

(Note: the shells shown are not precisely to scale with each other.)

1    2    3    4

The *GAU* committee commented that the gun could be assembled separately, because the fighting compartment was large enough to permit the whole gun to be fitted into the completed vehicle. It stipulated changes to the gun to enable a better rate of fire. The superstructure at the rear needed to be extended to match the size of the front superstructure plates, making room for a storage rack on the left side; a storage rack on the right side to be used by the breech block operator was to be added;

the gun was to have a sliding-wedge breech block; and fuel and oil cells needed to be relocated. The new gun with flaws sorted out needed to be approved on 20 March; however, delays meant it was only submitted on 17 April. The designers rejected an expansion of the fighting compartment. The Kirov Factory did report the loading tray for shells and cases needed to be raised, because it was difficult to feed propellant cases into the barrel; when the gun was traversed, the gunner or breech block operator found he had little room; and the ammunition rack was difficult to use. While these issues could not be resolved, a new sight based on the ST-10 was developed. This dispensed with parts causing problems with the sight's alignment and operation, and by doing so improved the image, as the system could be more properly centred. The sight would be used on both the SU-152 and the ISU-152.

The SU-152 was equipped with a liquid-cooled 600hp diesel engine. About 600–615 litres of fuel could be located in the fighting and engine compartments, with four external cylinders, two along each side of the engine compartment and not connected to the engine fuel system. Each could contain 90 litres of fuel. The internal fuel system was sufficient for 330km along roads and 165km on rough terrain. Eight gears forward and two reverse gears comprised the gearbox. On the road, 43km/hr could be achieved; off-road speed was 30km/hr. The ISU-152 was equipped with a liquid-cooled 520hp engine. Two fuel cells were located in the fighting compartment, with one in the engine compartment, carrying 520 litres, and four external tanks carrying 90 litres each. The range was 220km on the road and 145km on rough terrain. On the road, 35km/hr could be achieved; off-road speed was 15km/hr.

The 9P short wave radio the SU-152 used operated on a frequency range of 4–5.625MHz for transmitting and 3.75–6MHz for receiving. The extended range of the latter was intended for one-way communication with HQ. While the stationary range for voice communication could be 15–25km depending on interference, the range was slightly less while in motion. The radio could not use Morse code. There was also an intercom. The ISU-152 had either a 10P or 10RK radio operating on a frequency range of 3.75–6MHz for transmitting and receiving. The stationary range was 20–25km. Morse code could be used at longer ranges. The 10P allowed communication on two fixed frequencies without using a quartz resonator, while the 10RK enabled an easier selection of frequencies.

# GERMAN

Earlier Tiger designs had a 650hp Maybach engine. From spring 1943 a 700hp HL 230 TRM P45 23l Maybach engine was installed. The range was 120km on roads and 85km on firm ground, using 348 litres of fuel. Two 200-litre fuel cells could be carried on the back deck for long road marches. British trials noted that the Tiger could manage 21.5mph (34.6km/hr) on roads and 15mph (24km/hr) off road when the engine was measured, providing 592hp. The suspension comprised torsion bars running the width of the hull. The bars connected to road wheel arms, each of which had three wheels, overlapping wheels from adjacent wheel arms, creating a pattern that spread the load of the Tiger onto the track. A smooth ride was provided by hydraulic

The original Tiger paint colour was grey, although early examples on the Eastern Front would be white washed. In early 1943, 502nd Heavy Panzer Battalion had a mix of white and grey wedge shapes left exposed. In the spring, camouflage paint schemes would be used. From late summer 1943, Zimmerit paste (a chemical formula that prevented the adherence of magnetic mines) was painted onto the Tigers in the factory prior to camouflage being applied at the front. (Nik Cornish at www.Stavka.org.uk)

The Tiger's complex design needed extensive maintenance to keep it operational. If a Tiger engine broke, another Tiger was generally required to tow it. The workshop company had 18-ton tractors, though two were needed to tow a Tiger. The armoured *Bergepanther* was issued to Tiger battalions in 1944. There were never enough. The problems associated with recovering a Tiger would result in many abandoned vehicles being destroyed by their crews. Following the Kursk offensive in July 1943, three Tiger battalions would deploy to southern Russia to support the battalion there. However, they would often be deployed piecemeal. The commander of 506th Heavy Panzer Battalion, Major Willing, described his Tigers as having been pushed hither and thither to counter Soviet armoured breakthroughs, leading to damaged engines. Within seven days, none of the 45 Tigers would be operational, with only six lost to direct hits from enemy weapons. Also the Soviets would attempt to immobilize the Tigers with hits to the hull. (Keystone-France/Gamma-Keystone via Getty Images)

shock absorbers fitted to the front and back road wheel arms. Early production models had wheels with rubber rims; these would be replaced by metal road wheels in January 1944. New tracks with cast cleats for extra traction in the snow would be introduced from October 1943. Ten spare track links and pins would be carried in a container at the back of the turret. Spare links would be carried on the lower front hull plate and later on fittings welded onto the side of the turret.

To his right the commander had a manually operated wheel to rotate the turret, a single degree per two rotations. The commander decided whether to engage the target, and he was told to make rapid decisions based on good observation of the battlefield. The powered controls to operate the turret rotation had to be low geared because of the 120mm armour on the turret front, and thus they were slow, taking 60 seconds to rotate 360 degrees. Another wheel to the right of the gunner controlled the elevation of the main gun. A large spring housed in a cylinder on the left side of the turret compensated for the weight of the gun tube.

# TIGER AMMUNITION

The projectile and cartridge case were fixed. The *Pzgr Patr* weighed 14.97kg. The time of flight to 1,000m was 1.25secs at 800m/s. A pointed ballistic cap to streamline the round covered the nose, and the round was termed APCBC (Armour Piercing Cap Ballistic Cap) by British intelligence. The *Pzgr* 39 (**1**) was similar to the *Pzgr Patr*, with velocities of 773m/s. The *Pzgr* 40 round (**2**) weighed 13.8kg and had a tungsten carbide slug weighing 1.93kg. By 1943, because of the Allied blockade, production ceased and the rounds would only be used in dire emergencies. The *Gr Patr* 39 *HI* was a shaped-charge projectile, fired at 600m/s, capable of forming a high temperature jet to burn its way through armour upon target impact. The centrifugal effects rifling imparted on the projectile lessened the high temperature jet as it formed. Still, the Tiger used them, as 90mm of armour could be penetrated at ranges of 1,000m. The accuracy of the shot at the longer ranges was not as good as the *Pzgr Patr* 39. The Germans mentioned basic data on the armour penetration capabilities of the gun. The *Pzgr* 39 could penetrate 120mm of armour at 100m, decreased to 100mm at 1,000m. The *Pzgr* 40 could penetrate 170mm at 100m, decreasing to 138mm at 1,000m. These refer to armour set at 30 degrees from the perpendicular. At 2,000m, the *Pzgr* 39 could penetrate 64mm, and the *Pzgr* 40 could penetrate 110mm.

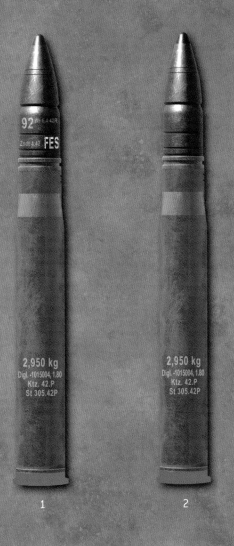

1     2

The Tiger's 8.8cm *KwK* L/56 used the 8.8cm *Sprgr Patr* HE round, the 8.8cm *Pzgr Patr* 39, plus small numbers of the 8.8cm *Pzgr Patr* 40 and *Gr Patr* 39 *HI* shaped charge. Two-thirds would be armour piercing. The life of the 8.8cm barrel was given as 6,000 rounds. The 8.8cm gun had a one-piece barrel in a thin jacket. Priming was electrical rather than percussion. A C/22 electrical primer took its power from the vehicle battery. The breech block slid vertically. Two hydraulic recoil mechanism cylinders were attached to the sides of the main gun tube, the recoil buffer on the right and the recuperator on the left.

The co-axial MG 34 7.92mm machine gun in the gun mantlet was operated by a floor pedal and could be fired at from minus eight degrees to plus 15. A second MG 34, ball mounted and located on the right side of the hull, was capable of 15 degrees traverse left or right and elevation of minus seven to plus 20 degrees. The machine gun was fitted with a *KZF* 2 sighting telescope capable of 1.75 magnification. Some 4,500 rounds were initially supplied for the machine guns, 4,800 by February 1944. An MG 34 could be carried on the turret, also fitted to the command Tiger.

The TZF was a binocular sight with 2.5 magnification. The commander had a turret position indicator. He operated a 10 SF 14Z stereo binocular sight and EM 34 range finder, increasing the range to 4,000m. A target 1,000m distant measuring 2.5m x 2m would be hit 100 per cent of the time, at 2,000m 87 per cent, and at 3,000m 53 per cent. A British test on a target moving at 15mph (24km/hr) at 1,500yd (1,370m) achieved 60 per cent success using low-speed gun laying. High-speed traverse reduced accuracy. Elevation angle ranged from plus 16 to minus seven degrees. Ammunition was stowed using four racks of 16 rounds (50/50 mix of AP/HE), four racks of four rounds (AP) and two racks of six rounds (AP). The Tiger command tank would have 66 rounds.

Tigers had a *FuG* 5 to communicate with other Tigers; the platoon commander also had a *FuG* 2. Command Tigers had *FuG* 5 and either a *FuG* 7 to communicate with Army commanders or a *FuG* 8 to communicate with the Luftwaffe. They had the turret MG removed and the aperture was filled with

The *TurmZielFernrohr* (turret sighting telescope or *TZF* – housed in the two apertures on the right of the gun mantlet) 9b or 9c was used for direct fire at targets. The no less effective TZF 9c required only a single aperture in the mantlet. On early mantlets, these two apertures resulted in weakened armour protection of 70mm. (Nik Cornish at www.Stavka.org.uk)

a plug. The command Tigers had the *FuG* 5 in the turret and the antenna for the *FuG* 8 for communication with higher HQ attached to the hull. The *FuG* 8 could transmit at 30W and had a star antenna. The *FuG* 7 radio did not possess the star antenna.

The Tiger had a circular escape hatch on the left rear of the turret and machine pistol port on the right rear. The turret roof armour increased from 26mm on September 1943 models to 45mm on later models from spring 1944. The commander's cupola was

When opened, the Tiger commander's cupola hatch projected upward, drawing enemy attention. The new low-profile cupola introduced in July 1943 pivoted horizontally when opened, saving many commanders from being killed, as the hatch was less noticeable and less of a target. The commander could sit on the upper seat and look out over the cupola or sit on the lower seat and look through the vision ports in the side of the cupola. (ullstein bild via Getty Images)

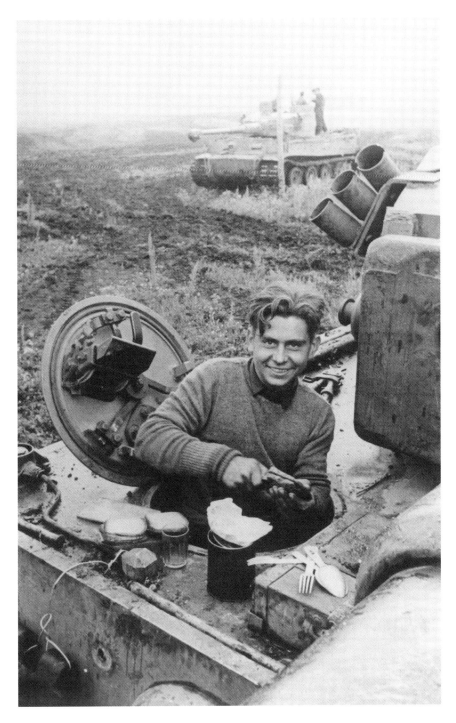

Smoke grenade launchers (two sets of three, each side of the turret – in the upper right of this photo), fitted in 1942, would be dispensed with by the summer of 1943, because they could be set off by enemy fire, thus temporarily blinding the crew. Instead, from March 1944, a close defence system called the *Nahverteidigungswaffe* was fitted. This fired a *Sprenggranate Patrone 326 Lp* a distance of 7–10m, exploding in mid-air to keep enemy infantry 100m from the Tiger. Smoke rounds could also be fired. This Tiger crewman operated a *Funkgerät* (*FuG*) 5 radio. In order for him to be able to exit through the hatch, the main gun tube needed to be out of the way, because the hatch swung upward rather than to the side. (Photo by Heinrich Hoffmann/ullstein bild via Getty Images)

modified to accommodate the thicker armour. Front turret armour set at 90 degrees was 97mm; turret side set at 90 degrees was 82mm, as was the turret rear and hull armour. Upper hull front armour set at 80 degrees was 102mm, lower hull front armour set at 70 degrees was 102mm; upper hull side armour set at 90 degrees was 82mm, lower hull side armour set at 90 degrees was 62mm. Glacis front armour set at 10 degrees was 62mm.

# THE COMBATANTS

## SOVIET

On 16 March 1943, 16 SU-152 regiments were formed numbered 1529 and 1535–1549. Self-propelled artillery units (*SAP*s) were initially formed with six batteries of two SU-152s, a KV-1S for the commander, a reconnaissance unit of four BA-64s and 42 support trucks. In July 1943, ten SU-152s of the newly formed 1549th *SAP* had to be replaced because of mechanical problems prior to going to the front. On 22 July,

Tiger crews fully appreciated the ISU-152's ability to take on German armour. The blast effect from its HE shell was often enough to blow the turret off a Tiger. A direct hit on the hull usually destroyed or damaged the tracks or suspension, immobilizing the vehicle. The round could also cause injuries through armour splintering (spalling) or blast concussion. Crews hit by the shell frequently abandoned their Tigers when this happened. (Nik Cornish at www.Stavka.org.uk)

the formation was complete, although only 50 per cent of trucks had arrived. 1549th *SAP* was assigned to 5th Guards Tank Army. In October, *SAP*s would be organized into four batteries of three SU-152s instead of six batteries of two SU-152s. By February 1944, this had changed to four batteries of five with an SU-152 for the commander.

The 1536th *SAP* was issued with SU-152s in April 1943 at Chelyabinsk. By 1 May, it had been issued with the KV-1S command vehicle, the BA-64 reconnaissance cars and three recovery tractors in Moscow. On 26 May, with 28 support vehicles along with three tractors, 1536th *SAP* arrived with 50th Army, where it was briefed on German armour tactics. In July it participated in the attack on Sukhinichi and lost two SPGs in the minefields. In August it recaptured Karachev, however only six SPGs remained operational. By September, a completely new complement of SU-152s was needed; training continued until the end of the year. By January 1944, it was with 59th Army. Along with 29th Tank Brigade and 65th Rifle Division, it raided enemy lines through forests and swamps near Luga, pulling out T-34s when they were stuck in the mud. The German defence was unhinged by this manoeuvre. The unit departed the line in March and was given ISU-152s. The SU-152s would be given to independent heavy tank regiments. 1536th *SAP* was renamed 378th *TSAP* and given a sub-machine gun (SMG) company, a technical support company, a sapper platoon and a command platoon. It was ready to deploy in early June.

Guards Major Sankovsky's 336th *TSAP*, established on 28 February 1944, would be equipped with ISU-152s. In the next three months, equipment arrived and the personnel carried out training. An SMG company and sapper platoon were added. Most of the ISU-152 crews were new recruits, having trained with 33rd Tank Regiment at Chelyabinsk. The gun commanders were mostly former political workers sent to military schools for 3 to 9 months. With the exception of mechanics, a large portion

The added protection of the ISU armour gave the ISU-152 the protection it needed to operate against most German AT guns. The ISU-152 could be used in the direct fire role more often, because most AP rounds could not penetrate its armour. German tanks with 75mm AT guns would not be able to penetrate, except perhaps at close range and in the side. The Tiger with its 88mm gun needed to close to medium range. This exposed it to the 85mm guns on the T-34/85, though not the 76mm gun on the T-34/76, unless, as suggested by this image, it targeted side armour. The low rate of fire was a problem in a meeting engagement. To compensate, the ISU-152 crew had to use camouflage, a battery's worth of guns firing at the side armour of a single target, then quickly deploy to another position. (From the fonds of the *RGAKFD* in Krasnogorsk via Stavka)

Commanders soon realized the importance of being able to use large, low-velocity HE rounds in cities against heavily fortified enemy positions, when they would deploy 200m behind the attacking tanks. Support to armour was the priority, though. The percentage of armoured crews to artillery crews was considered when recruiting personnel. Armoured commanders were mostly appointed to command positions, because the SPGs were seen as integral support to armour units. German artillerymen initially operating the Ferdinand SPG equipped with 8.8cm gun at Kursk in July 1943 suffered heavily because they would not work closely enough with their armour. (From the fonds of the *RGAKFD* in Krasnogorsk via Stavka)

of the replacements had no combat experience. On 1 July 1944 the unit was offloaded from train cars and started a 120km road march in the swampy, sandy soil of the Baltic. A platoon of scouts and the sappers had already prepared the route by reinforcing the roads. Regular halts were made in order to inspect and clean air filters. The new engines had to be broken in with great care, though only a single ISU-152 had to be abandoned, because the engine had burnt out. Another road march was ordered on 5 July, this time 150km on especially poor, winding roads through swampy terrain. The march started on the evening of 7 July; along the way another ISU-152's engine burnt out and three others had their engines repaired and worn-out tracks replaced. The inspection of the repairs at the assembly point, once they crawled in, showed new engines for these three would be needed. Yet another 150km move by 14 July resulted in two ISU-152s swapping old engines for new. By 17 July, 14 ISUs were available. A fourth march, of 180km, brought the unit to the front at the cost of another ISU-152. Two weeks of marches, covering 620km, meant eight ISU-152s could not be committed to battle. Sankovsky reported the engines of the ISU-152 built prior to May 1944 had weak oiling systems, which caused their engines to break after 50 hours of use. In July, 105 engine hours were expended. Sankovsky stated ISU-152s should be brought much closer to the frontline by rail and not be forced on exhausting road marches.

In February and March 1944, 398th *TSAP* was involved in the battle for Krivoi Rog and experienced issues with its SU-152s as well. The regiment had marched 1,200km and the early spring thaw had decimated 75 per cent of the wheeled component. The regiment went into reserve on 17 March, and while wheeled vehicles were mended in-house, a base repair unit mended a KV-1S, four SU-85s and eight SU-152s. The men studied how to operate in roadless terrain and, on 25 May, the regiment was loaded onto railcars and sent to the front, where 37th Army was based near Tiraspol. A 60km road march was difficult; the commander, Lieutenant Colonel Vetrov, would conclude that the base repair facility's work on his SU-152s was careless in many respects. Without exception, the engines overheated en route and the radiators filled up with dirt. A forgotten wrench, and nuts and bolts, were discovered in one radiator, and suspension components had not been serviced. The large backlash in the road wheels and the absence of grease in the wheels led to overheating during movement and premature wear of the working parts. Breakages of the steering clutch happened because the clutches were tightened too much at the repair base. Some entrenching blades, spare parts for the engines and guns, tow cables and shields were missing. The gun crews had to inspect all their equipment and mechanisms and correct deficiencies found.

The commander of 398th *TSAP* also noted deficiencies with the 152mm gun. Sometimes the casing would not extract properly after the round was fired. The longer the crew took to extract the casing, the more difficult the task became. Sometimes manual extraction was needed or the use of an extracting tool. Brass-cased rounds not cleaned of oil and dust properly or covered with corrosion because of poor ammunition storage practices could also be difficult to extract. If the casing had dents or scratches because the crew kept them improperly stowed in the hull or at the back wall of the crew compartment (not uncommon, as the crews wanted to take extra rounds into battle), off-road movement in particular caused them to knock against each other or fall onto the hull floor. Failure to extract was again a common problem. The best way to correct this deficiency was to extract as soon as firing had occurred.

A delay in firing the round was experienced when the breech failed to close properly, which was caused by the striking of the bar of the mechanism used to fill the recoil mechanism with oil. This deficiency occurred when the SP guns carried out long marches in dry, hot summers without a tarpaulin covering the breech. When the gun was fired frequently at full charge, sometimes the breech block would be wedged. The primer cup might not be in the proper position in the shell case, resulting in the breech

The SU-85 (on the right of this photo, with an SU-85M at left) replaced the 122mm gun on the SU-122 with the D-5T 85mm AT gun, built in May 1943. The first versions issued to the front from late summer did not have a commander's cupola. The gun, of which 2,660 would be produced, was capable of penetrating a Tiger at 1,000m. They could be issued to *SAP*s and could also equip AT units of the tank corps. (Courtesy of the Central Museum of the Armed Forces, Moscow via Stavka)

not closing properly, as the most forward position could not be reached; this could lead to casings striking the crew. In other instances, misfires could happen if the primer was screwed into the incorrect distance. To stop these deficiencies, the commander needed to demand that workers inspect ammunition prior to shells being sent forward.

Crews would complain that the designated stowage positions for ammunition were located in such inconvenient places that a metal bar was needed to reach them; this reduced the speed with which rounds could be loaded. The trigger was also criticized. The gunner had to disconnect the trigger from the previous firing in order for it to function; this caused him to lose temporary sight of his target. To eliminate this problem, a new trigger was recommended so as to allow the gunner to make his successive shot without interrupting his view through the sight. Another design deficiency was the need to unscrew three bolts on the gun mount in order to fire, if the crews kept the gun in travel position, as they frequently did. This disrupted the ability of crews to respond to ambushes or surprise attacks.

When the commander used the optical sight to observe the battlefield, in rain the sight would fog up and he would have to resort to the vision block in the roof hatch, subjecting himself to the risk of being struck by bullets or shrapnel. Also the seams of the components were not sealed with the proper compound. Crews recommended careful monitoring of the installation of optical instruments and the installation on the superstructure roof of a small command cupola with four vision scopes and panoramic scope. The poor functioning of the torsion springs on the crew compartment hatches was also noted; they frequently failed on abrupt opening. The escape hatch was another unfortunate issue, as its location was not helpful. In a combat situation, crews frequently had to abandon burning vehicles not through the escape hatch, but instead using the crew compartment hatches, a process that led to losses from enemy fire.

The majority of the enlisted component of 398th *TSAP* had experienced combat; however, the replacements from the tank regiments were poorly trained. Gunners were insufficiently trained in observing targets on the battlefield and determining range to

When the second company of 502nd Heavy Panzer Battalion was sent to southern Russia and incorporated as the third company of 503rd Heavy Panzer Battalion in January 1943, 502nd Heavy Panzer Battalion formed another second company in France with men from Pz Regt 3. Also, a third company was formed from Pz Regt 4. By July, these companies would be united with the first company to support Army Group North. Personnel for the Tiger battalions would often be experienced panzer crewmen with a wealth of experience in Poland, France and Russia. Heavy Panzer Replacement Training Battalion 500, established in Paderborn in early 1942, also provided many recruits. At Paderborn, training would often be on Pz IVs, because of the shortage of Tigers. Recruits to replace losses would usually be volunteers, aged 17 or 18 years old. Losses, because of the high protection offered by the Tiger's armour, would be low in comparison with those of other formations. (ullstein bild via Getty Images)

them with optical instruments; they adjusted fire poorly and they were unable to raise the zero line of the sight independently. The loaders and rammers poorly appreciated the technical components of the gun, especially the breech block, and could not correct minor stoppages by themselves. These deficiencies received intense attention in the course of exercises from June to mid-August 1944, so that the functional requirements of the crew members were brought to a level of automatic response. To reinforce their theoretical knowledge and to increase their appreciation of combined operations, the staff organized seven exercises, three with live rounds. In the middle of August, the regiment had a mix of 20 SU-152s and ISU-152s; however, the sapper platoon was missing and the SMG company was at 70 per cent strength.

# GERMAN

Originally, the Tiger companies of the first Tiger battalion would be organized with three platoons, each with three Tigers. On 15 August 1942, a mix of two Tigers and two medium Pz IIIs was authorized to equip four instead of three platoons. Company HQ comprised a Tiger and two Pz IIIs. The battalion also had an HQ and Supply Company, including, among others, a light platoon of five Pz IIIs, an engineer platoon, motorcycle platoon, and signal platoon. The Tiger battalion was to have three

In 1943, many personnel would be taken from panzer units destroyed in combat that were back in Germany or from panzer units rotating from other theatres. Sometimes whole battalions would be designated to be Tiger battalions. For example, III/Pz Regt 9, which had served in the Soviet Union since the start of that campaign, would become 506th Heavy Panzer Battalion on 20 July 1943. Elements of Pz Regt 4 from 13th Panzer Division would form 507th Heavy Panzer Battalion. The 1st Battalion, Pz Regt 29, would form 508th Heavy Panzer Battalion. Morale would be high, especially in units with prior status. Seen here is a Tiger crew sorting out kit. (Photo by Heinrich Hoffmann/ullstein bild via Getty Images)

Prior to Kursk, Tigers would not be employed en masse to create a breakthrough to be exploited by other armoured units; instead they would be used in small numbers as parts of combined arms groupings. These deployments, in the north and near Rostov in the south, provided excellent results in the winter of 1942/43, especially in the south, when German armies needed to withdraw from the Caucasus. In January 1943, with 2/502nd attached to 503rd Heavy Panzer Battalion, three companies were available. Deployed in platoon or company-size formations, the Tigers supported other formations defending the railways around Rostov. In two months of combat, 71 enemy armoured vehicles were knocked out for the loss of three Tigers and 13 Pz IIIs to enemy action. Another four Tigers would be sent back to Germany for major repairs. Just a single Tiger was destroyed deliberately at a railway station to avoid its capture. The large distances covered meant that the battalion had only 35 per cent operational strength. (Photo by Heinrich Hoffmann/ullstein bild via Getty Images)

companies of Tigers; however, shortages meant no battalion organized with the Company Organization D would muster a third Tiger company. A workshop company completed the battalion organization.

Another two heavy Tiger battalions with Company Organization D would be created by January 1943. On 5 March, the Army General Staff issued a new organization, forming a heavy Tiger company of three platoons of four tanks each, and two Tigers in the company HQ. The number of platoons was reduced from four to three. The battalion was to have three companies. The workshop company increased to three platoons and one recovery platoon. The light platoon was done away with; in its place a scout platoon with motorcycles helped a platoon of armoured infantry provide early warning of enemy attacks. The engineer platoon had three armoured engineer sections to clear mines and other obstacles. This organization authorized 45 Tigers for the battalion.

With 75 Tigers being produced every month and the intention to produce 125, four Tiger battalions adopted this organization (the other two were in Tunisia with two companies each) by July 1943. Three more battalions would be operational in September 1943, and the two lost in Tunisia would be re-established. In the spring of 1943, Pz Regt *Grossdeutschland* from PGD *GD*, with the company of Tigers already on its books and the third Tiger companies of 501st and 504th battalions, established a Tiger battalion. The battalion never had its full complement of Tigers, because it was in almost constant combat. The last Tiger battalion to be organized, 510th, was created on 6 June 1944, deploying to the Eastern Front immediately. The *Liebstandarte*, *Das Reich* and *Totenkopf SS* Panzer divisions had Tiger companies as part of their panzer regiments from the spring of 1943. Both 101st and 102nd *SS* Heavy Panzer battalions would be formed from the *Liebstandarte* and *Das Reich* Tiger companies. Operational in the spring of 1944, they would be assigned to I and II *SS* PC. 103rd *SS* Heavy Panzer Battalion would only fight in the last months of the war, as *Totenkopf* kept its Tiger company.

Doctrine on the deployment of Tigers was initially limited, following general tactical employment guidelines featured in memoranda written by the *General der Schnell Truppen*. The lighter tanks would lead and deploy to the flanks once they

Tigers would be kept together on the northern flank of the Kursk salient, assigned to an infantry division from a panzer corps carrying out the breakthrough attack. The 503rd Heavy Panzer Battalion was parcelled out on the southern flank with a company initially going to each panzer division. On 5 July, when the attack commenced, 13 of 14 Tigers of 2nd Company (Coy) would be immobilized by mines. It took three days to cover 20km. On 7 July, the Tiger battalion would be brought together to spearhead the attack to link with I SS PC; but it could not do this before the intervention of 5th Guards Tank Army on 12 July. Still, in the battle the Tiger battalion destroyed 72 T-34s for the loss of only four Tigers. The operational rate was 57 per cent. (ullstein bild via Getty Images)

North of Kursk, with less armour, on 5 July 1943 *Generaloberst* Model decided to attack with infantry forces and not commit his armour. The attack succeeded in breaking the Soviet line; however, 2nd Panzer Division was not available on the day to exploit the success. The Soviets brought reinforcements to the threatened area. The Tigers engaged them, destroying 109 T-34s in two days. When the Soviets launched their counter-attack on 15 and 17 July, the Tigers destroyed 54 T-34s. Three Tigers would be lost in the offensive battles and two in the defensive battles. From 4 to 20 July, 45.6 per cent would be operational. (ullstein bild via Getty Images)

encountered enemy armour, in order to allow the Tigers to engage. By 20 May 1943, tactical manuals for the employment of heavy tanks had been issued. Primary capabilities included the destruction of the first line of strong enemy fortifications, the destruction of enemy armour from long range and the breaking of heavily defended positions. The formations available to the platoon were the column, line, double column and wedge. The wedge was preferred in the attack. The company could either deploy in column with three platoons in column abreast, double column with the platoons in two columns, wedge with one platoon forward and the other two following, or broad wedge with two platoons forward and one platoon following. The broad wedge was thought to be the most useful in the attack; the company would be deployed in a formation 700m wide and 400m deep. The emphasis was on taking on enemy armour by attacking; no mention was made of the Tiger in the defence.

The battalion manual was shorter and focused on purposes, tasks and organization and employment. The battalion needed to be concentrated to be most effective. The battalions were designed to be Army troops, deployed to achieve a decision at the decisive point and not to be used on secondary tasks. They were expected to seek a battle with heavy enemy armour. They were not to be assigned missions lighter armour or assault guns could carry out. The manual did not address the tactical movement of the battalion together.

The General Inspectorate of Armoured Troops published a 25-point pamphlet for senior generals to guide them on the proper use of Tigers. The limited range meant

Shown here is a command Pz III. The Pz IIIs provided close support against infantry and helped destroy enemy AT guns. The first three Tiger battalions would have ten Pz IIIs, not five, in the light platoon. The light company could guard the battalion's flank or support against infantry attacks. The Tiger Company of *SS* Pz Regt 3 formed in late 1942 needed the soldiers from the armoured reconnaissance platoons of the Pz Regt to bring the company up to strength. These crews did four weeks on the Pz III prior to 14 days on the Tiger. They deployed shortly afterwards to Russia. The inclusion of Pz IIIs lasted until May 1943. Company commanders were free to decide the best way to combine Pz IIIs and Tigers. The German Tiger commanders mostly wanted to keep the Pz III, though the commander of the Tiger Company of the PGD *GD* thought they needed complicated maintenance, because Pz III parts needed to be brought along. *Generaloberst* Guderian was happy to lose them. (ullstein bild via Getty Images)

commanders would have to maintain close liaison with Tigers, providing movement orders as early as possible. Tigers needed to be at the point of main effort and never be subordinated to an infantry division in the attack, because the infantry did not have enough assets to keep pace with the Tigers. The likelihood of mechanical problems was addressed. Tigers needed to be given the opportunity to move without changing gears, so as to protect automotive parts. If Tigers broke down, they could disturb the movement of other formations. Tigers should not use forced marches, because of the wear on the engine transmission and gears, as they needed to conserve combat capability for battle. The average speed of the Tiger was assessed to be 10km/hr in the

The Tigers at Kursk would be depleted because of mechanical problems caused by mines, enemy hits and terrain obstacles. Fuel consumption would be high if used at the point of the attack, with a lack of fuel for the decisive battle. Guderian, who had had experience of the Kursk battles, would say placing the Tigers up front was wasteful, because they would not possess sufficient combat power later on when the decisive battle would be fought. He did, however, reject a proposal from *Grossdeutschland* to provide a Tiger platoon to every panzer battalion. (ullstein bild via Getty Images)

day and 7km/hr in the dark. Tigers needed two to three weeks to restore fighting power following prolonged combat; otherwise technical deficiencies would climb steeply. The correct positioning of the Tiger battalion to respond to enemy attacks was essential to mount counter-attacks on enemy armour effectively, especially in the larger operational environment of the Eastern Front.

A total of six independent Tiger battalions with the Tiger battalion of PGD *GD* were on the Eastern Front by the end of May 1944. With the German Army conducting a fighting withdrawal, Tigers suffering from mechanical failure could not be so easily brought away. By the end of July, three would be decimated by the Soviet summer offensive. Only 501st Heavy Panzer Battalion with 20 Tigers was with Army Group Centre when Operation *Bagration* started in June. Within two weeks the battalion, deployed to Orsha, was destroyed north-east of Minsk, despite a reinforcement of five new Tigers. In the summer of 1944, three Tiger battalions defended Lithuania and East Prussia, and two were in Poland. In Germany, three battalions were given King Tigers. Up to the spring of 1945, the Tigers of PGD *GD*, 502nd, 507th and 510th Heavy Panzer battalions all fought in northern Germany, Poland, East Prussia or Kurland. In January 1945, 507th Heavy Panzer Battalion, still operating Tigers, was part of XXIV PC and was effective in destroying enemy-armoured spearheads, losing only four Tigers to combat. Withdrawal commenced on 19 January. All 22 Tigers that reached the Vistula on 30 January had to be destroyed, because there were no ferries to take them across.

# COMBAT

## BELGOROD–KHARKOV OFFENSIVE, AUGUST 1943

On 3 August 1943, following Germany's failed attempt to break the Soviet line at Kursk, the Soviet Steppe and Voronezh fronts launched an offensive to encircle Kharkov from the north and west with M. Katukov's 1st TA and P. Rotmistrov's 5th GTA, plus two additional MCs. Four tank corps would make supporting attacks. The line between Army Detachment Kempf and Fourth Panzer Army was soon broken when Belgorod was captured. Kharkov was bypassed to the north and the Soviets swung south-west heading toward the Dnepr. On 12 August, 2nd *SS* Panzer Division *Das Reich* and 3rd *SS* Panzer Division *Totenkopf* arrived from a deployment further south to near Bogodukhov, 30km north-west of Kharkov, to stop the Soviets from surrounding Kempf in Kharkov. By occupying ambush positions, 3rd and 4th batteries of 1549th *SAP* destroyed seven German tanks, including three Tigers. German aircraft were called in and one SU-152 was destroyed. By the next day, three SU-152s had been lost because of engine trouble and seven others needed major repair. When the last two suffered engine problems on 15 August, the unit was out of action completely; however, by 22 August, nine were brought back to operational capability in time for the next attack on *Das Reich*. Both 5th *SS* Panzer Division *Wiking* and 3rd *SS* Panzer Division *Totenkopf* had stood on the defence east of Bogodukhov, supported by *Das Reich*, while *Totenkopf* and PGD *GD* moved on 27th Army, supported by 6th Guards Army near Krasnokutsk, cutting them off and forcing them to withdraw temporarily. However, 5th GTA could not be stopped

1529th *SAP* arrived with 7th Guards Army on 30 May 1943 with 270 personnel, including 67 officers, 74 NCOs and 129 privates. On 8 July, in the Kursk offensive, the army commander, Lieutenant General Shumilov, visited the unit and expressed gratitude at the way enemy armour was targeted. No. 3 Battery had set two on fire and hit another two, including a Tiger, from a company attached to 7th Panzer Division. The commander, Major Dormakov, had been a forward observer for howitzers belonging to an infantry division earlier in the war. He was decorated for destroying eight Tigers in August near Korotich. (From the fonds of the *RGAKFD* in Krasnogorsk via Stavka)

from moving on Korotich to cut the Poltava–Kharkov rail line, which was defended by *Das Reich* and *Wiking*.

On 21–22 August, 18th Tank Corps from 5th GTA engaged *Das Reich* in a successful attack on Hill 123.1, on their way to Korotich. By the evening they were on the outskirts with 5th GMC. The Germans needed to leave Kharkov and launched a successful counter-attack on Korotich on 23 August. On the same day, 1549th *SAP* was ordered to Korotich, making a 72km night march. *Wiking* elements had occupied Korotich, especially the Poltava–Kharkov rail embankment. The next day, 5th GTA lost 39 tanks storming the embankment. On 25 August, 1549th *SAP* reported Lieutenant Bogatyrev (3rd Battery Commander) destroying a Tiger, two SU-152s of 5th Battery destroying two Tigers, and 4th Battery destroying another Tiger, whilst

supporting 32nd TB at Korotich. The regiment lost three SU-152s evacuated from the battlefield. Three men were killed and seven wounded. On a rainy 26 August, a German counter-attack with four Tigers, supported by Panzergrenadiers, was defeated by 1549th *SAP* and elements of 25th Tank Brigade with the loss of three tanks. The cost was 42 T-34s destroyed. By 28 August, *Das Reich* had only six Tigers and 24 Panthers in working order. Still, they counter-attacked in the morning in poor visibility, according to 1549th *SAP*, with the loss of three Tigers and two damaged. By the end of the day, 5th GTA had 50 operational tanks. In the evening of the following day, the Germans pulled back to a new position.

On 26 August, ten SU-152s of 1529th *SAP*, together with the T-34s of 5th GMC, prepared to attack Kommunar state farm. A German company with two Tigers, probably from *Das Reich*, was detected prior to the attack. At 0730hrs, two groups of five SU-152s advanced in the fog. At ranges of between 200 and 300m, the 152mm guns swept away buildings and soon one of the Tigers was burning. The farm was occupied, however, without infantry support, and by the evening the unit had to withdraw to its former positions. The next day, at 1430hrs, the SU-152s again occupied the farm, destroying two Pz IVs. Although Soviet infantry arrived in the evening, they quickly moved further forward, leaving the SP guns once again on their own. A German counter-attack at dusk with infantry and Tigers was effective. The infantry highlighted the SU-152s with tracer bullets for the Tigers. The Germans destroyed four SU-152s. In total, 1529th *SAP* lost eight SU-152s in two days, seven burnt and one sent for factory repair. The last four SU-152s, along with their crews, would be given to 1548th *SAP* on 9 September.

German aircraft would prioritize the identification and destruction of SU-152s. As part of 3rd GMC of Voronezh Front, 1831st *TSAP* went into the Belgorod battle in August 1943, supporting 8th GMB. The attempt to advance on Chupakhovka

5th GTA lost 450 tanks and SP guns in August. The Tigers had survived Kursk and were able to provide a solid defence following the battle. Here, a Tiger is seen ready to engage Soviet armour somewhere in southern Russia following the battle of Kursk. (Keystone-France/Gamma-Keystone via Getty Images)

In late July 1943, 1538th *TSAP* had seven SU-152s and one KV-1S, and was attached to 82nd Tank Regiment during Operation *Kutuzov* to seize Orel. On 24 July, the regiment was operationally subordinated to 283rd Rifle Division of Bryansk Front with six operational SU-152s and four being repaired. On 30 July, supporting the division in fighting for the fortified village of Shumovo, the SP guns suppressed the fire of three Pz IVs and two Tigers with no loss. On 1 August, equipment was received from the reorganization of 1452nd *SAP* and ten SU-122s were assigned to the regiment; in the next week or so, maintenance issues kept the operational strength low and no combat was experienced until mid-September. 1538th *SAP*, renamed 374th *TSAP*, was equipped with ISU-152s in February 1944 and would fight with 4th Tank Army. (Nik Cornish at www.Stavka.org.uk)

On 1 September 1943, 1831st *SAP* was brought to help 3rd GMC. The SU-152s supported 35th GTB and three Tigers were destroyed for the loss of one SU-152 near Kholodny. The enemy was located in defensive positions in Yanovshchina (Gogolevo). The unit commander, Lieutenant Colonel Kulikov, was wounded in fierce fighting from 2–5 September. Owing to equipment issues, especially those associated with the filters, 1831st *TSAP* needed a breather. On 28 February 1944, 343rd *TSAP* was formed from 1831st *SAP* with ISU-152s joining 5th Army of 3rd Belorussian Front for Operation *Bagration* in June 1944. (Courtesy of the Central Museum of the Armed Forces, Moscow via Stavka)

initially failed because of intense German artillery barrages; 1831st *TSAP* then occupied a defensive line near Pyatkin from 22 to 25 August. German planes targeted the SU-152s; only when the Germans moved back from their positions did 3rd GMC launch a pursuit. On 26 August, a strong German armoured force struck 7th GMB in the flank at Levchenka and it had to withdraw; 1831st *TSAP* was used to support 30th Rifle Division, while 23rd Rifle Corps was being attacked by German armour. Enemy planes targeted the SU-152s, setting two ablaze, though in both instances the fires were extinguished.

While advancing on the Poltava–Kharkov rail line, 1549th *SAP* continued to experience heavy losses. On 1 September, a battalion of 25th Tank Brigade, with three SU-152s, commanded by Lieutenant Bulavitsy, was ambushed while advancing on Ogultsy. Once clear of the embankment, the T-34s were soon knocked out along with a company of infantry accompanying them. Bulavitsy was killed when he went on a foot reconnaissance to see what had happened to the T-34s. Two Panzer IVs and seven Tigers with infantry support then moved on the SU-152s. Lieutenant Kobozev, the senior surviving officer, with no orders to retreat and out of ammunition, decided to stay. All three SU-152s were soon burning wrecks. Kobozev's crew escaped on foot. He attempted to recover his SPGs at night; however,

the Germans destroyed them completely. The attack had cost the Germans as well, with three Tigers and two Pz IVs also burning. In addition, seven SU-152s needed major repair; five of them needed new engines. The unit claimed ten Pz IVs and 15 Tigers destroyed in a month of continuous fighting. The claims of Tigers destroyed are probably inaccurate, with SU-152 crews reporting Pz IVs with *schuerzen* as Tigers. German sources do report three Tigers lost due to enemy fire by *Das Reich*, though do not specify the cause.

# KRIVOI ROG, OCTOBER 1943

The Soviets pushed over the Dnieper River at Kremenchug and Zaporozhye in the first week of October. On the 15th, six armies pushed out of Kremenchug and punched a hole between Wohler's Eighth Army and General Hans-Valentin Hube's First Panzer Army. From 5 September to 14 October, 1549th *SAP* was refitting and training, and had received a full complement of vehicles by 17 October. However, when it was called upon to support 5th GTA on 22 October, four were not operational for unspecified technical reasons. 5th GTA with 7th GMC was launched from the Dnieper bridgehead toward Krivoi Rog on 15 October. On 18 October, 5th GTA was close to the city, and raided its outskirts on 23 October. It could not take the city and

The Soviet armour of 5th GTA headed straight for Krivoi Rog, the communications, supply and rail centre for Army Group South. The loss of enormous supply dumps and considerable quantities of locomotives, plus rolling stock, threatened to deal a disabling blow to Army Group South's power to resist. The Tigers of PGD *GD* and *Totenkopf* would launch successful counter-attacks to keep the Soviets out of the city. (Presse-Illustr. Hoffmann/ullstein bild via Getty Images)

was thrown back by German panzer forces brought into the area. 1549th *SAP* moved
forward to assist in the defence of the ore mines near Krivoi Rog; despite preparations
to operate from concealed positions, aircraft targeted 1549th *SAP*, wounding three
lieutenants among others. German aircraft were close to the combat zone and proved
effective.

On 24 October, the commander's KV-1S and five SU-152s were near the chemical
plant and ore works north-west of Krivoi Rog. From ambush positions, two other
batteries supported two tank brigades of 5th GTA that had suffered heavy losses.
Lieutenant Bogatyrev with his 2nd Battery destroyed two Tigers near Vesely Kut. The
crew of one 4th Battery SU-152 claimed a Tiger destroyed on 28 October. Elements
of PGD *GD*, 3rd *SS* Panzer Division with 16th and 24th Panzer divisions were part
of the counter-attacking force. *Grossdeutschland* had 23 Tigers in action near Krivoi
Rog on 20 October, losing seven in a day and a further seven by the end of the month.

A German counter-offensive attempted to encircle Soviet forces north-west of
Krivoi Rog on 30 October. Following orders, 1549th *SAP* withdrew, and in doing so,
the KV-1S and three SU-152s were destroyed to prevent the Germans from seizing
them. While being repaired, two others had to be disabled by breaking the engine
blocks. The remaining SU-152s closely supported the T-34s on 1 November when the
German counter-attack continued. German aircraft were actively targeting them; only
five SU-152s remained serviceable when, on 5 November, all SU-152s were given to
a repair base for a week. Krivoi Rog would only be liberated on 22 February 1944.

On 14 November, 32nd Tank Brigade supported by 1549th *SAP* would attack
elements of 71st Infantry Division on high ground, supported by a tank battalion.

The height was successfully taken and the Germans launched five Tigers with Panzergrenadiers and close air support to throw the Soviets off the position. Lieutenant Smyshlyaev's SU-152 knocked out a Tiger, however his vehicle was struck in the hull and destroyed. Lieutenant Khoteyev also knocked out a Tiger; and then his SU-152 was also destroyed. The German attack was beaten off with the loss of four Tigers burnt and two damaged. Four SU-152s were left. Equipped with Tigers, 9th Coy of *SS* Pz Regt 3 participated in the attack on 32nd Tank Brigade, wrecking 28 T-34s near Batschtina, though no Tigers were recorded as lost. The Tigers claimed by 1549th *SAP* could instead be Panzer IVs with *schuerzen*. Of the SU-152s lost, five could not be repaired. Losses included 17 killed, including five officers, and 20 wounded. On 16 March, the personnel began a 15-day training programme, and 1549th *SAP* was renamed 339th *TSAP*. On 7 April, the crews departed for Chelyabinsk, where they were issued with their new ISU-152s.

# ROTMISTRIVKA, JANUARY 1944

In late January 1944, the Tiger battalion and Panther battalion led by *Major* Franz Bäke operated successfully against Soviet armoured spearheads north of Cherkassy

Although the Tiger Company from 1st *SS Liebstandarte* Panzer Division was supposed to have 14 Tigers, only four would be operational when they attacked Soviet positions near Rotmistrivka on 25 January 1944. On the left of this Tiger crew photo is Michael Wittmann, a Tiger platoon commander, awarded the *Ritterkreuz* in early January and recommended for the Oakleaves soon after, prior to the attack on Rotmistrivka. (Photo by Heinrich Hoffmann/ullstein bild via Getty Images)

prior to the encirclement of German forces there. *Kampfgruppe* (*KG*) Kuhlmann, the commander of the Panther battalion of Pz Regt *LSSAH* south of Rotmistrivka, would attempt to join up with Bäke's heavy regiment. The Tiger Company of *LSSAH* was in the lead and would advance to Hill 316.6 near Otscheretjna. The SU-152s of 1548th *SAP* supported elements of 100th Tank Brigade and 65th MRB from 1st Tank Army. On 24 January, when the German attack commenced, the brigade commander decided to use the SU-152s to try to stop them on the outskirts of Rotmistrivka. Of three SU-152s in 3rd Battery, one was sent off because of a maintenance issue, and Tigers fired upon the other two prior to firing positions being occupied. The SU-152 crews responded and set one Tiger on fire; however, rounds from the Tiger forced the two crews to abandon their vehicles. Standing in covered positions behind a railway track, 2nd Battery spotted a column of German tanks at less than 1,000m and opened fire. Two Tigers were struck and shortly thereafter a barrage of fire descended on them. Then 4th Battery opened fire at 1,500m at enemy armour. When the enemy tanks pivoted toward the threat, SU-85s and T-34s also fired at them, dispersing the Germans as they sought refuge.

By the afternoon, five SU-152s, seven SU-85s and one T-34 of 15th GTR and 20 T-34s from 20th GTR were assembled in northern Rotmistrivka, supporting the infantry of 20th MB. Two AT batteries were also incorporated into the defence. German *SS* armour battle groups again moved on Rotmistrivka. They suppressed the AT guns and moved on the T-34s, destroying two and forcing the remainder to lower ground. The Tigers claimed the railway embankment to obtain a better line of sight and were then seen by the SU-152s. The Tigers quickly reversed back, taking a damaged Tiger with them. On 26 January, Lieutenant Krasnousov, with five SU-152s, was now isolated from the rest of the regiment. With no ammunition or fuel, he decided to abandon them and lead the crews back to his regiment. With the arrival of a new tank formation, the defensive situation improved and the regiment could recover the abandoned vehicles. One SU-152 had to be towed and the batteries took six hours to cover 8km.

# CHERKASSY, JANUARY–FEBRUARY 1944

On 25 January 1944, to the south of 1st Tank Army, General Konev's 2nd Ukrainian Front, with 5th GTA (218 tanks plus 18 SP guns), having captured Kirovgrad, was south of the German force still on the Dnieper near Kanev. Vatutin's 1st Ukrainian Front with 6th Tank Army was north of the Kanev bulge. Both would advance to encircle the Germans by linking at Zvenigorodka, 75km and 50km from the front line, respectively. The 5th GTA's 20th Tank Corps (8th GTB, 155th Tank Brigade and 80th Tank Brigade) had 1895th and 1834th *SAP*. They were followed by 18th Tank Corps with 29th Tank Corps. The encirclement was complete by 28 January. With 326 tanks and SP guns, 2nd GTA was brought forward on the northern flank to defend the encirclement from German counter-attacks.

On 4 February, Bäke led 16th and 17th Panzer divisions of III PC to break the Soviet encirclement. On 5 February, he used Panthers to go around the flank of Soviet armour while Tigers engaged frontally from long range. A Soviet tank brigade was smashed with no German losses. The 5th GTC from 6th Tank Army with 1832nd *SAP* was brought forward to support what remained of 2nd GTA's 3rd and 16th Tank corps (1540th *SAP* and 1542nd *SAP*). The 5th GMC from 6th Tank Army had 1827th *SAP* in support. On 12 February, Bäke encountered 5th GTC and 20th Tank Corps in defensive positions north of Frankovka. Panthers went around the flank and Tigers engaged frontally again, destroying 80 Soviet vehicles and 50 AT guns. Four Panthers and four Tigers were lost. Bäke linked around Hill 239 with 1st Panzer Division elements on 15 February; he only had nine operational Tigers. Eight Tigers stormed the hill on 17 February, escorting German forces out of the pocket. Of the 56,000 encircled forces, 30,000 would be saved. Bäke lost 22 Tigers.

# NEZVISKO, APRIL 1944

The Soviets launched an offensive on 4 March 1944, taking them to the foothills of the Carpathians, isolating parts of Army Group South and forcing the Germans to use poorly maintained supply lines in the Balkans. General Georgiy Zhukov's 1st

The German attack to break the encirclement of the Cherkassy pocket stalled because of the mud. The supply company only had about 60 per cent of its wheeled vehicles operational and this led to maintenance issues. Fuel had to be brought long distances without the use of paved roads and Tigers had limited ammunition. Also, the encircled forces moved further east because of Soviet pressure and the need to shorten the line. The sole combat officer in Bäke's Tiger battalion took command of the Tigers, forming four platoons. 506th Heavy Panzer Battalion was then assigned to Bäke; in theory it had 27 Tigers, though probably only a company's worth could fight. (Courtesy of the Central Museum of the Armed Forces, Moscow via Stavka)

At Nezvisko, 30 Panthers had advanced; one company was stuck in mines and the other two present had engaged the ISU-152s; 15 were lost. The Tiger of *Stabsfeldwebel* Liechauer belonging to 2nd/506th supporting them was ambushed and knocked out by an ISU-152. The commander and gunner were killed, but the loader remained in the Tiger. He was wounded when a 122mm shell from an IS-2 struck his tank. *Oberleutnant* Brandt, CO of 2nd/506th, was killed when his Tiger was hit by an ISU-152 as his company moved south-east. The next day, five Tigers with the Panthers seized Hill 32, though all the Tigers had mechanical problems and two could not be brought out. (Courtesy of the Central Museum of the Armed Forces, Moscow via Stavka)

Ukrainian Front surrounded Hube's First Panzer Army at Kamenets Podolsk, forcing the Germans to deploy II *SS* PC from France to liberate them. The 1st Tank Army was not able to defend the encirclement, because Katukov had gone toward the Carpathians, covering 170km in two weeks. In April he only had 50 operational tanks and needed the support of his SPGs. The Germans brought forward Tigers of 2nd/506th and the Panther battalion of Pz Regt 23 to northern Bukovina. On 20 April 1944, at Nezvisko, 399th *TSAP* (16 ISU-152s), commanded by Colonel D. Kobrin, plus 72nd GHTR equipped with ten IS-2s, encountered them. However, many SPGs would be lost partly because the crews had not learnt to change positions quickly enough. Zhukov would criticize Katukov for committing the SP guns because of the heavy losses, until he observed for himself the damage they had done.

Kobrin wrote about the engagement. The 399th *TSAP* had only had the ISU-152s since 13 April. With only six days to train, the crews had had a single gunnery practice prior to being sent to the front. Battery commanders reported not having enough familiarity with their crews. By the evening, they had marched 65km to 47th Rifle Corps. On 14 April they supported 167th Rifle Division, helping guard against enemy counter-attacks on 15 and 16 April. A 200km march ensued on 17 April prior to the regiment being positioned on approach routes enemy armour was expected to take. One battery covered three others on the approach to Nezvisko. By 1230hrs on 20 April, these three opened fire at ranges of 1,200–1,400m on German armour. Tigers and Panthers used folds in the ground and ravines to close the range. The reserve battery was successfully thrown in to defend Hill 302 on the left. Kobrin claimed nine enemy tanks burnt and seven destroyed; however, 12 ISU-152s were burnt as well. Five ISU-152s were operational on 21 and 22 April, in position to repel German armour. Kobrin spoke of a low rate of fire and insufficient accuracy, no rest prior to the battle and lack of time to prepare. No infantry or armour was available to protect the ISU-152s. The crews fought to the last and did not retreat, command and control by radio from the commander worked, the use of a reserve was decisive and the ability to march 200km without suffering mechanical failure meant the regiment was at full strength prior to the battle.

# TARGUS FRUMOS, APRIL–JUNE 1944

On 5 April 1944, while the Kamenets Podolsk battle was still being fought, 2nd Ukrainian Front commanded by Konev attacked the upper reaches of the Dniester River in north-east Romania with 2nd Tank Army and 6th Tank Army. Facing him was *Generaloberst* Schorner's *Heeresgruppe Sud Ukraine* with Sixth and Eighth armies, plus Third and Fourth Romanian armies. The 2nd Tank Army began to breach enemy defences near Targus Frumos; simultaneously 6th Tank Army launched a supporting attack north of Jassy. The spring thaw then significantly slowed the advance.

The Tigers of PGD *GD* numbered as few as eight operational on 30 April 1944, perhaps less on 2 May, perhaps more. The *Totenkopf* Tiger Coy, fighting with *GD* Tigers, had three Tigers on 2 May. In total, *GD* had a company's worth of Tigers. *GD* also had about 20 Panthers plus about 22 Pz IVs. *Totenkopf* also committed 20 Pz IVs to the battle. *GD* would receive eight Tigers on 6 May following the battle. (ullstein bild via Getty Images)

The Germans reacted quickly and threw *GD* into battle, commanded by *Generalleutnant* von Manteuffel, near Targus Frumos. The 1st Romanian Guards Armoured Division and 7th Romanian Infantry Division attacked from the south, forcing the Soviets to abandon the town. On 2 May, Konev began another offensive against German and Romanian defences north of Targus Frumos, and this time 375th *TSAP* was included, along with part of 3rd Tank Corps from 2nd Tank Army, supporting 57th MRB. The Germans had LII PC with *GD*, *Totenkopf* and 24th Panzer Division, supporting Fourth Romanian Army. Manteuffel kept most of his armour in reserve.

On the morning of 2 May, 2nd Tank Army moved on *GD* with 200–250 armoured vehicles. The Panzergrenadiers tried in vain to hold their positions; many occupied them for too long and would be cut down by Soviet soldiers while attempting to surrender; however, the Soviet armour was outstripping the infantry. The Germans counter-attacked with three Tigers and Panzergrenadiers supported by artillery and mortars, pushing the Soviets to the northern slope of Hill 197.0. Tigers mainly duelled with IS tanks from long range, letting Pz IVs close to within 1km.

The 375th *TSAP* ISU-152s claimed damage to a Tiger and discouraged the Germans from making further progress. The ISU-152s then advanced to the northern slope and supported the infantry's seizure of Hill 256, a mile further south. Late on 2 May, *GD* Tigers and Panthers moved forward to directly support the *GD* infantry the next day. On 3 May, 375th *TSAP*, with the order to support three tank brigade attacks on the Targus Frumos road, had to advance on another hill; however, effective fire from towed artillery plus tanks from *GD* and ground attack planes halted the Soviet armour. One ISU-152 was burnt out by an aerial bomb hit. The 3rd Tank Corps began to withdraw, with its commander, Lieutenant General Mishulin, ordering 375th *TSAP* to stem the German pursuit. Another German air raid, now with three squadrons, with heavy artillery and mortar support, was conducted prior to a counter-attack on 375th *TSAP* positions by three Tigers, joined by a company of armour from three directions. One wounded commander with two sub-machine gunners doused the fire on his ISU-152 and then infantrymen assisted him in the SPG by loading shells; they destroyed a Tiger, but were hit again and set on fire. The 3rd Battery commander skilfully directed his ISU-152s. When an ISU-152 commander was killed, the battery commander took his place and brought his battery forward in order to engage from close range. He gave the order to fire and with his first shots set two Tigers ablaze. At the end of the day, the ISU-152s were occupying positions near Hill 256. Nine ISU-152s were burned out. Four other ISU-152s needed to be evacuated from the battlefield for repair.

The Germans persistently attacked 375th *TSAP* positions from 4–5 May, eventually occupying Hill 256 on 7 May. With seven ISU-152s, 375th *TSAP* could be brought out of the line for equipment repair, combat training and political instruction for its enlisted component. The regiment claimed eight Tigers destroyed in the battle. The Germans only admitted to ten armoured vehicles destroyed in *GD*. The Soviets had 350 tanks destroyed. Schneider records no losses of Tigers from *GD* or *Totenkopf*.

The Germans persisted with their counter-attacks. On 2 June, when 375th *TSAP* was back in the line, 30–50 German tanks, probably from *GD*, supported an infantry attack on 206th Rifle Division. Seven ISU-152s occupied reverse slope positions and claimed a Tiger and Panzer IV destroyed. On 7 June, 375th *TSAP* supported the attack by 107th Tank Brigade on Moynisshtiy. Once the armour had reached the northern part of the settlement, aircraft-supported German armour pushed them out. Again, the ISU-152s were used to discourage further German advances, claiming two Panthers and two Tigers destroyed or damaged. Two ISU-152s set ablaze by enemy fire were repaired at the maintenance collection point. The next day the unit reported another two Tigers burnt out when the Germans attacked. *GD* was still at the front and could have engaged 375th *TSAP* in these battles prior to transportation by rail to East Prussia.

# PLESKAU, APRIL 1944

The Soviets commenced the Leningrad–Novgorod operation in January 1944, and by March had pushed the Germans from positions south of Leningrad, throwing them back 220–280km and inflicting heavy losses on Army Group North. The Germans, however, had successfully pulled back to the Panther Line, a system of defences north and south of Lake Peipus, inflicting, according to official Soviet accounts, nearly 77,000 killed, missing or captured on three Soviet fronts, and 237,000 wounded or sick. The Leningrad Front's 42nd, 54th and 67th armies continued the offensive against Pleskau in early March. The Supreme Command expected Pleskau to be liberated by 10 March. On 1 March, 46th Rifle Division from 110th Rifle Corps of 67th Army moved forward, and in three days advanced only 10km to the fortifications of the Panther Line. The next objective in late March would be the Pleskau–Ostrov railway and road; 67th Army would then move on the Velikaya River.

1539th *SAP* was formed in April 1943 and deployed to the front in July, attached to 68th Tank Brigade of the Bryansk Front. After reorganization in October 1943, the unit deployed to 2nd Baltic Front and by February 1944 had an SMG company and sapper platoon prior to operating with 29th GHTR in 10th Guards Army. They then fought in the Rezhetsko–Dvina operation with 207th Rifle Division at Rundeni from 18 to 20 July. Named 373rd *TSAP* on 17 July, they were equipped with ISU-152s in August. The 373rd *TSAP* was attached to 3rd Belorussian Front and seized Dünaburg (Daugavpils). Guards Captain F. Nagovitsyn, a battery commander, is seen here giving orders to Lieutenant S.F. Berezin. (From the fonds of the *RGAKFD* in Krasnogorsk via Stavka)

The German positions in front of 402nd Rifle Regiment, 168th Rifle Division, 67th Army, had two trench lines with dugouts, machine gun platforms, and earth bunkers; however, there was no barbed wire or minefields. The 168th Rifle Division, supported by 1902nd *SAP*, liberated Podborovye. At nearby Morkova, at 1330hrs, two Tigers and two StuG IIIs supported a German infantry attack launched with artillery support, isolating the settlement. 1st Battalion, 402nd Rifle Regiment retreated. At 1500hrs, a second attack by infantry and two Tigers pressured the new positions, forcing them back another 400m. The 2nd Battalion, 402nd Rifle Regiment held off a company of infantry with StuG III support, before being forced to retreat. No SU-152s were committed. (ullstein bild via Getty Images)

**OPPOSITE**

Staroselye and Bolshyye Usy, 3–8 April 1944.

The 67th Army (98th, 110th and 108th Rifle corps) and 42nd Army (118th and 123rd Rifle corps) would target German units south of Pleskau, supported by two light SP artillery regiments plus 31st GHTR and 36th GHTR, equipped with 20 tanks, three SU-85, three SU-122, 43 SU-76 and four SU-152. To the south of 67th Army, 7th, 111th and 119th Rifle corps from 54th Army started their offensive on 31 March when 7th Rifle Corps moved from Sidorovo against 212th Infantry Division. The next day, 310th Rifle Division from 7th Rifle Corps occupied Vernyavino and 65th Rifle Division Volkovo. Rapid German counter-attacks by 212th Infantry Division with five StuG IIIs and two Tigers threw them out of both. They were also supported by a panzer *kampfgruppe* based on I/Pz Gren Regt 25 with armour of company strength (Pz IIIs and IVs). With the onset of darkness, 310th Rifle Division reported assaulting into the flank of German infantry supported by Tigers as they advanced toward Voronino. The panzer *kampfgruppe* was more successful, forcing the Soviets out of the village. The commander of 54th Army noted the need for layered AT defences, including the use of 76mm guns from the artillery regiments.

On 2 April, 239th Rifle Division, 7th Rifle Corps occupied a portion of the Pleskau–Ostrov road north-east of Vadrino. However, 65th Rifle Division could not capture Suslovo, and 310th Rifle Division, with three regiments deployed, could not capture Vernyavino. The Soviets also moved on Vadrino; when the infantry went to ground, the four armoured vehicles supporting them pressed on and broke through German defences, only to be destroyed by StuGs. The 54th Army then received 108th Rifle Corps from 67th Army. The 239th Rifle Division was reinforced by four KV-1s and six SU-152s from 33rd GHTR, and SU-76s from 1197th *SAP*, located at Koroveyo Selo.

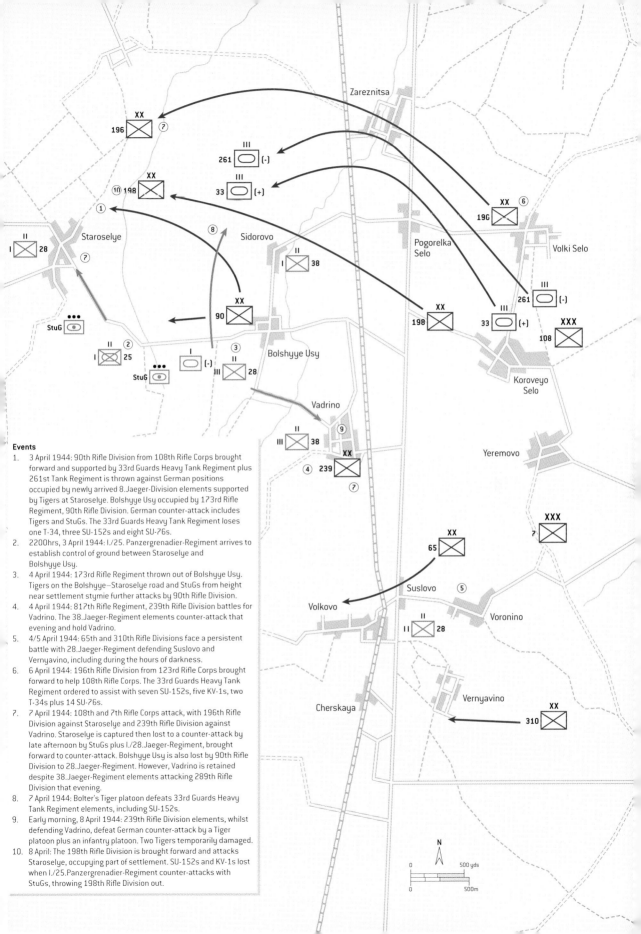

Zareznitsa

XX 196 ?

III 261 (-)

III 33 (+)

XX 198 ⑩

① Staroselye

XX 19G ⑥

Volki Selo

II I 28 ?

Sidorovo

Pogorelka Selo

II I 38

⑧

III 261 (-)

XX 198

III 33 (+)

XXX 108

XX 90

StuG •••

II I 25 ②

I (-) III II 28 ③

Bolshyye Usy

Koroveyo Selo

StuG •••

Vadrino

⑨

XX 239 ④

⑦

Yeremovo

II III 38

XXX ?

XX 65

Suslovo ⑤

Volkovo

Voronino

II II 28

Cherskaya

Vernyavino

XX 310

**Events**

1. 3 April 1944: 90th Rifle Division from 108th Rifle Corps brought forward and supported by 33rd Guards Heavy Tank Regiment plus 261st Tank Regiment is thrown against German positions occupied by newly arrived 8.Jaeger-Division elements supported by Tigers at Staroselye. Bolshyye Usy occupied by 173rd Rifle Regiment, 90th Rifle Division. German counter-attack includes Tigers and StuGs. The 33rd Guards Heavy Tank Regiment loses one T-34, three SU-152s and eight SU-76s.

2. 2200hrs, 3 April 1944: I./25.Panzergrenadier-Regiment arrives to establish control of ground between Staroselye and Bolshyye Usy.

3. 4 April 1944: 173rd Rifle Regiment thrown out of Bolshyye Usy. Tigers on the Bolshyye–Staroselye road and StuGs from height near settlement stymie further attacks by 90th Rifle Division.

4. 4 April 1944: 817th Rifle Regiment, 239th Rifle Division battles for Vadrino. The 38.Jaeger-Regiment elements counter-attack that evening and hold Vadrino.

5. 4/5 April 1944: 65th and 310th Rifle Divisions face a persistent battle with 28.Jaeger-Regiment defending Suslovo and Vernyavino, including during the hours of darkness.

6. 6 April 1944: 196th Rifle Division from 123rd Rifle Corps brought forward to help 108th Rifle Corps. The 33rd Guards Heavy Tank Regiment ordered to assist with seven SU-152s, five KV-1s, two T-34s plus 14 SU-76s.

7. 7 April 1944: 108th and 7th Rifle Corps attack, with 196th Rifle Division against Staroselye and 239th Rifle Division against Vadrino. Staroselye is captured then lost to a counter-attack by late afternoon by StuGs plus I./28.Jaeger-Regiment, brought forward to counter-attack. Bolshyye Usy is also lost by 90th Rifle Division to 28.Jaeger-Regiment. However, Vadrino is retained despite 38.Jaeger-Regiment elements attacking 289th Rifle Division that evening.

8. 7 April 1944: Bolter's Tiger platoon defeats 33rd Guards Heavy Tank Regiment elements, including SU-152s.

9. Early morning, 8 April 1944: 239th Rifle Division elements, whilst defending Vadrino, defeat German counter-attack by a Tiger platoon plus an infantry platoon. Two Tigers temporarily damaged.

10. 8 April: The 198th Rifle Division is brought forward and attacks Staroselye, occupying part of settlement. SU-152s and KV-1s lost when I./25.Panzergrenadier-Regiment counter-attacks with StuGs, throwing 198th Rifle Division out.

N

0          500 yds

0          500m

On 3 April, the newly arrived 108th Rifle Corps was thrown across the Pleskau–Ostrov road. 38th Jaeger Regiment, with two battalions and two from 28th Jaeger Regiment, had only just taken the positions vacated by 212th Infantry Division. Three artillery battalions were also brought forward. Some 502nd Heavy Panzer Battalion Tigers would be subordinated to 8th Jaeger Division. The panzer *kampfgruppe* was withdrawn except for elements of 1st Battalion, 25th PG Regt. The 90th Rifle Division from 108th Rifle Corps with 173rd and 286th Rifle regiments, supported by armour and SPGs from 33rd GHTR, advanced 200–300m to the Staroselye–Bolshyye Usy road at 1300hrs. The 173rd Rifle Regiment occupied Bolshyye Usy and the Germans launched seven counter-attacks, each with a company reinforced by armour including StuGs and Tigers. Two German tanks were damaged. The Soviet armoured losses were noted; one T-34, three SU-152s and one SU-76. German reinforcements in the form of I/Pz Gren Regt 25 established control of the ground between Staroselye and Bolshyye Usy. The 108th Rifle Corps explained the failed Soviet attack by referring to the artillery bombardment not lasting long enough or not being strong enough. The German defenders found shelter and reappeared when the barrage lifted.

The 7th Rifle Corps attacked slightly to the south of 108th Rifle Corps. The 239th Rifle Division's 817th Regiment reached the road near Vadrino. The Germans used the railway embankment to stop any further advance. The 65th Rifle Division, attacking Suslovo, was unable to advance. The 310th Rifle Division elements (a platoon of 1080th Rifle Regiment) further south at 1445hrs burst into the north-east outskirts of Vernyavino and went to ground. The next day, having brought some guns forward, two regiments of 65th Rifle Division launched themselves on Suslovo, suffering heavy losses, because the Germans were hidden in deep trenches and permanent bunkers. Soviet artillery was insufficient and German armour hastened to the scene. The 65th Rifle Division had to be reformed with reinforcements.

During the early hours of 4 April, a company of infantry supported by armour, following a 30-minute bombardment, forced 173rd Rifle Regiment (90th Rifle Division) out of the northern outskirts of Bolshyye Usy. At 1000hrs, 286th Rifle Regiment and 1st Battalion, 19th Rifle Regiment could advance only 100–150m before going to ground, because of fire from an elevation to the west of Bolshyye Usy. Soviet sources state a platoon of five Tigers used the Staroselye–Bolshyye Usy road to fire on targets of opportunity from the move; another platoon of five Tigers was in stationary positions; and four Tigers were on the reverse slope of the elevation. 8th Jaeger Division reported the infantry attack in the afternoon on Bolshyye Usy was supported by armour. According to 108th Rifle Corps, the failure of the Soviet attacks was because the infantry commanders had no idea of how to combat German armour; the infantry and gun commanders did not work together.

To the south of Bolshyye Usy, 7th Rifle Corps launched two regiments of 239th Rifle Division on Vadrino at 1000hrs. The 817th Rifle Regiment made it across the railway embankment, going to ground soon thereafter. The 239th Rifle Division losses were 66 killed and 260 wounded. At 1515hrs, 8th Jaeger Division reported Vadrino had been lost. A German counter-attack was readied from the north and south and by 1550hrs was successful. The Soviets again retook the village and III/38th Jaeger Regiment again occupied Vadrino, at 1915hrs. At Vernyavino, elements from two regiments of 310th Rifle Division evicted the Germans that night.

A counter-attack early the next morning from three axes by 9/28th Jaeger Regiment and a platoon of armour was successful. The 65th Rifle Division decided to use the night of 4/5th to attack Suslovo by surprise; the Germans were fully prepared and illuminated them with rockets and decimated them with fire. A Soviet company leapt into trenches and both sides used grenades. The small company-size Soviet force was forced to withdraw.

The commander of 54th Army noted his attacking formations were unable to deal with mobile armoured groups that were moving freely and organizing ambushes to stall the Soviet offensive; he described the fundamental base of the German defence as armoured strong points covered by the organized fire of automatic weapons, guns and mortars, supported by planes. Armour could carry out almost uninterrupted attacks to support the defence line. The Soviets moved forces northward on 5 April; however, guns from 8th Jaeger Division disrupted them, forcing them instead to opt for unsuccessful night combat against Vadrino, Voronino and Naumykovo. 8th Jaeger Division credited guns and mortars with causing immense losses to the Soviet infantry. From 3 to 5 April, 54th Army lost 998 killed.

The dispatch of two German artillery battalions by army HQ on the night of 5/6 April weakened the 8th Jaeger Division defences. The Germans detected new Soviet formations, and on 6 April at 1900hrs, III/28th Jaeger Regiment elements with Tigers in support attempted to move east of Bolshyye Usy, to the rail line 1km north of Vadrino. Soviet guns and mortars brought them to a halt. The 8th Jaeger Division reported one Tiger was lost. The Soviets reported this German force at 1930hrs as five armoured vehicles moving south on Koroveyo Selo from Vadrino against elements of 239th Rifle Division. The artillery of 90th Rifle Division helped halt the German armour. A 122mm gun damaged a Tiger. Soviet sources state this Tiger was repaired by soldiers from 813th Rifle Regiment, 239th Rifle Division, and brought back to Soviet lines.

Other elements of 502nd Heavy Panzer Battalion supported the defensive line north of Lake Peipus. SU-152s again supported the Soviet offensive; the Tiger of *Oberleutnant* Carius was knocked out near Hill 312 by a probable SU-152. German engineers destroyed the Tiger, because recovery was not possible, as it was on the other side of a wide ditch. The psychological support the Tigers could give to the infantry sustained them despite the mechanical problems of operating in trackless, marshy ground. The Tiger company was redeployed in late April to Pleskau. Here, 502nd Heavy Panzer Battalion would gather once again. Personnel, including Hans Bölter, were sent on leave, of short duration once the next Soviet offensive began. (Nik Cornish at www.Stavka.org.uk)

A Soviet ISU-152 advances across the Neisse River into Germany in early 1945. (Public Domain)

The Soviets reorganized on 6 April. The 108th and 7th Rifle corps, each with two divisions in the first echelon, would strike on the right flank in order to get across the Velikaya. Subsequently, 119th Rifle Corps would be launched frontally; 196th Rifle Division from 123rd Rifle Corps was brought into 108th Rifle Corps; and 19th Rifle Regiment from 90th Rifle Division needed reorganizing and was out of the line. The commander of 90th Rifle Division was told to complete the organization of AT groups and ensure enough Molotov cocktails were distributed. Each soldier was also supposed to be issued with three to four AT grenades. Colonel Kislitsyn – commander of 33rd GHTR, which was subordinated to 108th Rifle Corps – was to get five KV-1s, seven SU-152s, two T-34s and 14 SU-76s.

Following a 50-minute bombardment, 108th and 7th Rifle corps went into the attack at 0800hrs on 7 April. Pinning attacks were launched by 111th and 119th Rifle corps. The commander of 108th Rifle Corps, Major General M. F. Tikhonov, ordered 196th Rifle Division to defeat the enemy at the Staroselye strong points and support the subsequent advance to the Velikaya River. Two regiments were in the first echelon. The 196th Rifle Division described fierce close combat in the trenches in Staroselye; by the afternoon, the attacking regiments had added their second echelon to the fray. By 1400hrs, the outskirts of Staroselye were occupied. The 8th Jaeger Division reported Staroselye being attacked by a battalion and seven armoured vehicles; 30 armoured vehicles also supported infantry attacking between Staroselye and Bolshyye Usy. StuG IIIs were ordered to the front. Forty-seven StuG IIIs with 500 AT shells were available; however, they took time to reach 8th Jaeger Division and so the Tigers had to be relied upon.

# HANS BÖLTER

Hans Bölter was born in 1915 and joined the army in 1933. He was first assigned to a motorized reconnaissance battalion, then 8/1st Panzer Regiment. In 1939, he was a sergeant commanding a Pz IV platoon in the Polish campaign. In the French campaign, he was often in the lead, supporting the reconnaissance group, destroying obstacles the French had in place, and was wounded. When he was back with his regiment in October, he was promoted to sergeant major.

Bölter's division invaded the Baltic States in June 1941, and in July he destroyed ten Soviet tanks; although his vehicle was knocked out, the crew survived. He was wounded again in October and would be sent back to Germany for treatment. In 1942 he was with the reserve battalion of 1st Panzer Division at Erfurt, training officer cadets. In order to gain promotion, he sought assignment to 502nd Heavy Panzer Battalion. He first commanded a platoon from 1st Coy, comprising two Tigers and three Pz IIIs. He supported 170th Infantry Division and 96th Infantry Division, the target of a Soviet offensive designed to break the siege of Leningrad. In one battle he destroyed seven T-34s. With his engine hit, the crew bailed out and Bölter managed to get out, despite shell fragments wounding him. He discharged himself from hospital within eight days. Later, in January 1943, he destroyed two KV-1s. The Soviet offensive had cleared a route into Leningrad south of Lake Ladoga. In February the 1st Coy (the others had gone to France) successfully supported the *SS* Flemish Legion when the next Soviet offensive began south of the corridor. Pressure intensified near Mga in March. For his part in these defensive battles, Bölter was promoted to *Leutnant*.

The 502nd Heavy Panzer Battalion assembled again in the spring, in time for the Soviet summer offensive. Positions were held with Tiger support. In April 1944, Bölter's 1st Coy fought near Pleskau and he was awarded the *Ritterkreuz*. For the summer battles, Bölter was promoted to *Oberleutnant* and would be awarded the Oak Leaves. He was sent to Paderborn, after being wounded, to instruct, and then to the NCO school at Eisenach. On 2 April 1945, 500th Training Battalion was made operational with personnel from the NCO school, with Bölter commanding 2nd Coy, which was composed of King Tigers. He ambushed US Shermans later that month in the Stecklenbach area. In another combat engagement with Shermans, Bölter's crew bailed out when the turret was hit. He dismissed his men and travelled to his home in Erfurt, in the Soviet occupation zone, in civilian clothing.

Bölter subsequently fled to West Germany and worked in a large industrial firm, passing away in 1967 at the age of 62. He had destroyed 139 tanks, the fourth highest of all tank aces.

*Oberleutnant* Bölter's Tiger platoon, of the 502nd Heavy Panzer Battalion, was told on the night of 6/7 April that it might be needed. However, it would only be brought to the front once the Soviets had made obvious the location of their main advance. Bölter was awakened early in the morning by the noise of diesel engines, so he decided to go to the infantry HQ of the Jaeger Regiment to see what was happening. Just as he reached the command post at 0600hrs, the Soviet offensive struck with hundreds of guns opening fire. After the frontline was saturated with shells, heavy Soviet artillery targeted beyond the main battle line, including the quarters of the Tiger crews. When Bölter rushed into the infantry command bunker, a shell hit a nearby barracks, destroying the wooden structure. A wounded courier opened the door of the command bunker and reported Soviet armour on the move. The bunker was being bombarded and only on the fourth attempt could Bölter and *Feldwebel* Göring exit the HQ safely.

Rockets landed close to the three Tigers as they moved forward. Then the bombardment stopped abruptly. Soviet infantry went into the attack. The Tiger crews looked for supporting Soviet armour. The armour with the initial infantry attack had halted and decided to go around the flank, where the German infantry lacked heavy weapons. Bölter knew little about this at first. He did, however, realize that Sperling's

Tiger, which had been struck by the bombardment, would be delayed. Only when a German infantryman was spotted and questioned did Bölter know Soviet armour had gone through the main battle line. Bölter ordered full speed. He soon noticed Soviet armour emerging from a wood behind the German trenches. He identified T-34s and KV-1s in the middle and SP guns travelling around the flanks to fire their 122mm and 152mm guns at the German infantry. Using fire and movement, Bölter and Göring took it in turns to close the range to 1,000m; soon four AFVs would be burning, as the Soviet crews could not lock onto the targets. This quickly gained the attention of the other vehicles.

A hail of fire was brought against the Tigers. Bölter's tank was hit and a brilliant light momentarily lit the interior. A loud bang was heard, the Tiger shuddered and smoke enveloped them; however, the Tiger survived because the Soviet gunner had hit the front armour. Bölter ordered a move into a hollow to the right and then into some cover. At the same time an SU-152 moved into his sights, halting and getting ready to fire. He ordered the Tiger to stop and the gunner to fire. His gunner Riedl pulled the firing lever. The SPG exploded. The movement to some shrubs resumed. Once in this cover, Riedl targeted the next AFV with a single shot, forcing it to grind to a halt. The shell case clattered out of the breech into the shell bag and Mühlhaus loaded the next round. Meanwhile, AFVs were rushing past at high speed on both sides 1,000m from them.

Bölter then heard a bang on the right side and could hear the grinding of the tracks unusually clearly. He decided to move off ahead. The tracks responded. He wondered how he was going to get out of this mess when suddenly a rumbling announced the arrival of Göring, who had temporarily withdrawn for repair and, with Sperling, had now reached the battlefield, charging past Bölter on both sides and pursuing the Soviet vehicles as they took flight, despite their superior numbers. Göring scored hits on four vehicles and Sperling on two SPGs. Sperling waited until the SU-152s had fired and then closed to within 600m. He knew the SU-152 loading time was greater than a minute. He knocked out two and hit another, causing the vehicle to smoke and withdraw into a forest.

Bölter observed new targets and ordered a quick move through hollows and over small elevations into a birch wood on his left. Although the wood was dense, he soon reached the other side, where he observed several AFVs some hundreds of metres from his position, their crews out of their vehicles discussing the situation. In two minutes Riedl fired three times and set three AFVs on fire before the others started to return fire. One round grazed Bölter's turret, so he ordered the Tiger back 30m. With shells landing around them, the Tiger escaped into the wood and then reached a large crater. The pursuers soon showed themselves and Riedl dispatched two and the others retreated. The Tiger heaved itself out of the shell hole, moving in a wide arc so Bölter could get a better view from his original position.

Once back on the rise, Bölter could see two AFVs move cautiously toward the wood 1,000m distant. The first shot hit one; a cloud of smoke obscured the wreck while the crew got onto the other AFV. The vehicle pivoted and hastily withdrew to their lines. Göring and Sperling rejoined Bölter. Göring reported his seventh hit. Sperling, who was on Bölter's left, was hit in the front by a 15.2cm shell before Bölter, dealing with an AFV also firing on Sperling, could help. The explosion tore open some armour; though capable of moving, the Tiger could not fight. The next hit would be decisive. Sperling reported to Bölter he had decided to clear off. Göring fired at the SU-152 and persuaded the crew to exit the battlefield.

Meanwhile, 7th Rifle Corps with 239th Rifle Division's 813th and 817th Rifle regiments had attacked Vadrino. By 1000hrs, 813th Rifle Regiment had taken the place by storm, despite the German counter bombardment and direct fire from four infantry guns. The third regiment was brought into Vadrino to help 813th Rifle Regiment in all round defence. III/38th Jaeger Regiment launched multiple counter-attacks supported by armour (Tigers and StuGs) in platoon strength in the afternoon and early evening. By the end of the day, all three 239th Rifle Division regiments were defending the buildings. German attacks in limited strength and scope persisted that night. The 239th Rifle Division lost 266 men, including 48 killed. At Staroselye, 196th Rifle Division had brought forward its 3rd Rifle Regiment. Despite this, the Germans retook the settlement in the late afternoon with StuGs, and I/28th Jaeger Regiment. By 1900hrs the Germans had taken Bolshyye Usy as well, and the Soviet start line was reached. The 196th Rifle Division had lost 99 killed, 90th Rifle Division 550 killed and wounded. From 3 to 8 April, 90th Rifle Division had lost 1,250 men, killed and wounded. The 65th Rifle Division had moved on Suslovo, going to ground 100m from the place, losing 81 killed and 290 wounded. In most instances, effective German artillery fire had disrupted Soviet infantry attacks.

On 8 April, 198th Rifle Division was brought into battle against Staroselye, occupying the northern portion with the Germans in the southern. *KG* Weber,

Tiger 211, camouflaged with foliage, in 1944. The Soviets bombarded 121st Infantry Division near Ostrov on 22 June. Bölter, commanding 3rd Coy, was ordered to move on the Pleskau–Ostrov railway along with 2nd Coy. The counter-attack commenced on 24 June; coordination between the Tigers and infantry was poor. 2nd Coy reached the crest of a hill and the Soviet bunker system before the infantry. Soviet artillery immobilized two Tigers. One was destroyed by German fire to stop the Soviets from capturing it; the other was towed away. The Tigers had to withdraw from the hill that evening. On 26 June the crest was attacked with artillery support. An SU-152 shell hit the turret of a Tiger from *Oberleutnant* Carius's company and another was hit and destroyed when it went over the crest. Two Soviet SU-152s were destroyed from 1,500m. (Nik Cornish at www.Stavka.org.uk)

defending the settlement, reported a KV-1S and SU-152 were damaged in the German counter-attack that threw the Soviets out. German counter-attacks with a platoon of Tigers in support pushed 239th Rifle Division to the eastern outskirts of Vadrino. At 0330hrs the next day, three Tigers with 50 infantry were repulsed and 239th Rifle Division reported a Tiger burnt. German sources report two Tigers damaged, one was repaired on the day, and the other needed longer. The 310th Rifle Division launched an offensive at Orekhova Gora and was rapidly counter-attacked, but the Soviets held the line. The 65th Rifle Division committed the 3rd Rifle Regiment to get astride the road between Suslovo and Vadrino. The 8th Jaeger Division noticed the Soviet advance was less intense, because of losses suffered on 7 April. The Soviets unsuccessfully used limited armour on Vadrino in the hours of darkness. The next day, the commander, 54th Army, decided to place 108th Rifle Corps in reserve and cease further attacks and 30th Infantry Division was brought in to replace 8th Jaeger Division.

# OPERATION *BAGRATION*, SUMMER 1944

In total, 14 heavy self-propelled artillery regiments (*TSAP*s) with ISU-152s would be assigned to the attacking fronts in June 1944 for Operation *Bagration*. The 333rd and 335th *TSAP* were part of 6th Guards Army, 43rd Army had 377th *TSAP*, and 336th and 346th *TSAP* had yet to be assigned by 1st Baltic Front. The 3rd Belorussian Front with infantry armies had 337th, 343rd, 395th, 345th and 348th *TSAP*, and 5th GTA had 376th *TSAP*. The 2nd Belorussian Front had 334th and 342nd *TSAP*. In total,

2.3 million men and 5,200 tanks opposed 1.2 million Germans with 800 tanks and 530 SP guns. The 3rd GTC of 5th GTA had 125 T-34s, plus 81 Shermans and Valentines; 19th GTB, 1436th *SAP* with SU-85s, 10th Guards Motorcycle Battalion (GMB), and one battery from 376th *TSAP* led 3rd GTC. They were ordered to liberate Borisov and stop the Germans near Orsha from escaping. The Fifth Army had already broken through enemy defences and the Germans were rushing 5th Panzer Division with 505th Heavy Panzer Battalion to the Krupki–Bobr area.

Shishkin's battery of 376th *TSAP* mostly operated with 19th GTB. The brigade commander, Grigory Pokhodzeev, ordered Shishkin to advance to destroy a Tiger after some of his T-34s were knocked out when they moved into a clearing from a nearby wood. His SU-152 started to climb the hillock with Shishkin leaning out of his hatch to catch a view of the Tiger. He observed the Tiger, with its stern by a large tree, fire at him and felt a whirlwind of air whoosh past his head. He noticed a bush on the hill. He aligned the bush with the crown of the tree. He lowered the gun and used its howitzer properties to fire his projectile, knocking out the Tiger. Meanwhile, 3rd GTC was ordered to liberate Borisov; instead of moving along the Minsk road, the SP guns moved in the forests and were used to destroy barricades when encountered. Shishkin was again wounded by a shell fragment and taken to a field hospital. The splinter was taken out and he was back with his unit within a week.

In late June 1944, the ISU-152s of 343rd *TSAP* assisted 2nd GTB in Skog and Bogushevsk on the way to Orsha. The 2nd GTB was already being helped by 395th *TSAP*, also equipped with ISU-152s and fully integrated with the T-34s and SU-85s. The 395th *TSAP*, prior to being re-equipped with ISU-152s in February 1944, was 9th GHTR. The StuG IVs from 95th Infantry Division in Skog ambushed the T-34s of 2nd GTB, setting fire to five. They then targeted the ISU-152s in their side armour, causing some losses. This is when eight ISU-152s from 343rd *TSAP* approached to deal with the German ambush. (Courtesy of the Central Museum of the Armed Forces, Moscow via Stavka)

On 27 June, 3rd GTB was stopped by five Tigers of 505th Heavy Panzer Battalion near the Bobr River, the T-34s finding refuge in a forest while the ISU-152 battery was brought forward. The ISU-152s of Senior Sergeants Andrei Gladyshev and Sergei Bychkov from 1st Battery and ISU-152 of Mikhail Gusev from 2nd Battery destroyed two bunkers and one Tiger. The SMG battalion of 3rd GTB crossed the river while being covered by T-34s, SU-85s and ISU-152s, and seized enemy trenches in Bobr. The 505th Heavy Panzer Battalion recorded knocking out 16 armoured vehicles on 27 June, prior to retreating to the forests to the north-west. On 28 June, as they were outflanked by 3rd GTC elements going around the forest, the Germans had to move out to Borisov, fighting a battle on the way at Krupki, captured by the Soviets in the evening. The 1/505th Heavy Panzer Battalion destroyed 17 tanks (505th claimed a total of 34) on 28 June.

Then 5th Panzer Division started to arrive near Borisov. On 29 June, 3rd GTC encountered armoured elements from 5th Panzer Division and 505th Heavy Panzer Battalion. The 18th GTB, with the support of two batteries of SU-85s from 1436th *SAP*, was ambushed. The German *kampfgruppe* had permitted the Soviets to go past them and then attacked. A group from 19th GTB with a battery from 376th *TSAP*, perhaps Shishkin's, was sent to help them, arriving the next day, limiting losses. Three Tigers were destroyed on 29 June. While the SMG battalion from 18th GTB could get into Borisov on 30 June, the armour could not and had to wait until a pontoon bridge was in place. The 3rd GTC was now at 50 per cent strength. Borisov was taken on 1 July. By 6 July, 5th GTA had lost 159 tanks and SPGs, approximately 50 per cent of its strength. 505th Heavy Panzer Battalion had lost nine Tigers. The Germans evacuated Borisov; however, 12 Tigers had to be blown up because they could not be retrieved on 7 July. Only four were operational, with 24 in repair.

# DÜNABURG (DAUGAVPILS/DVINSK)

The *Bagration* offensive created a huge gap between Army Groups North and Centre. The Soviet forces of 3rd Belorussian Front were already 50km south-east of the city, moving west on Siaulai, 100km south of Riga. The 2nd and 3rd companies of 502nd Heavy Panzer Battalion arrived on 4 July and deployed south-east of Dünaburg, the base of a new frontline. The only method to cross the Western Dvina River was the railway bridge in Dünaburg. No bridges could be used by Tigers for a distance of 100km either side, neither could they use fords. The 502nd Heavy Panzer Battalion's engineer platoon planned to position a 60-ton ferry north-west of Dünaburg. The 1st Baltic Front (4th SA, 6th Guards Army, 43rd Army) was approaching on both sides of the Western Dvina.

1st Coy arrived at Dünaburg with ten Tigers on 12 July. Five Tigers from 1st Coy, commanded by Bölter, reinforced 3rd Coy with 225th Infantry Division in Wensawai, south-west of Dünaburg. Five other Tigers from 1st Coy supported 81st Infantry Division at the Wazsaliena estate 20km east of Dünaburg. Here, on 16 July, AT guns knocked out three of *Oberleutnant* Baumann's five Tigers. Bölter, appointed commander of the Tigers with 225th Infantry Division, was ordered to move on the Wazsaliena estate; following an 80km march on the morning of 17 July, he attacked on 18 July toward Plauskiety with the support of 15 assault guns to help 189th GR. While the Tigers destroyed the AT guns, German infantry could not keep pace. Bölter had to pull back. Bölter was brought with Baumann to Sarasai to be the reserve. Four Tigers of 3rd Coy stayed with 225th Infantry Division. When the Soviets broke through the German lines north-east of Dünaburg with heavy armour on 20 July, the company was ordered to block the road 6km north of Komai. In the afternoon, two Tigers blocked enemy attacks between Romanetjzky and Schipy. They counter-attacked south of Rokiskis station; ISU-152s knocked both out.

Soviet forces attacked 290th Infantry Division 28km east of Dünaburg on 22 July. The 502nd Heavy Panzer Battalion, ordered north of the Western Dvina River to support them, would operate in a smaller area in terrain not permitting off-road movement. Bölter with 1st Coy destroyed six T-34/85s at Leikumi. Carius followed on with 2nd Coy, encountering heavy Soviet armour near Malinawa. The 290th Infantry Division was in danger of being encircled if the Soviets crossed the road to Rossitten. Carius, with eight Tigers, surprised a Soviet IS-2 battalion by charging into Krivani, destroying 17 IS-2s and five T-34s. The Soviet heavy armour battalion was

On 10 July, 3/502nd, whilst supporting an infantry battalion attack, lost two Tigers to AT gun shots 22km from Giarnai. Five vehicles broke down because of the heat and the 50km-long road march the previous day. The 2nd Coy was ordered to recover them at the pontoon bridge site at Deguizi; of the five Tigers it started with, two made it to 3rd Coy. With the five Tigers repaired, seven operational Tigers were ordered to Dünaburg, then Tarzeka, to support 215th Infantry Division elements. Two made it, and two from the workshops joined them. In three days, only four out of 22 Tigers were operational, albeit only temporarily. (Courtesy of the Central Museum of the Armed Forces, Moscow via Stavka)

From 24 June 1944, in two months, 17 Tigers from 502nd Heavy Panzer Battalion were destroyed or sent to Germany for repair, and 22 were repaired by the 502nd after being damaged by Soviet armour or guns. The forced marches of the Tigers in the summer heat in July meant spare parts were rapidly consumed. This occurred when the replacement parts depot was being moved from Riga to Königsberg on two freight cars; this move would take two weeks. Frequent gear slippage could result in damage to the transmission. The next losses were six Tigers on 14 September when the Riga offensive operation started, prior to the battalion moving back to Germany in October. (Nik Cornish at www.Stavka.org.uk)

waiting for reinforcements before continuing its advance on Dünaburg and many crews were plundering houses. Carius then positioned his Tigers to observe the road from concealed positions. They destroyed 28 armoured vehicles from a Soviet column as it advanced along the road.

The Soviets then prepared to advance on Dünaburg from the north-west. The new commander of 290th Infantry Division did not expect this approach. Carius convinced *Major* Schwaner to let him move a platoon to cover the Riga road to allow the Dünaburg garrison to pull out prior to encirclement. On 24 July, six of *Leutnant* Nienstadt's Tigers knocked out 17 armoured vehicles (including two SU-122s) at close range on the Rositten road; a 152mm round, possibly from 326th *TSAP*, destroyed a Tiger. Carius had already been wounded while carrying out reconnaissance near the Riga road. On each day from 22–26 July, small groups of Tigers blunted Soviet armoured spearheads, destroying 73 armoured vehicles and 24 guns while losing only four Tigers, delaying the capture of Dünaburg to 27 July when 6th Guards Army of 2nd Baltic Front took the city. In early August, Bölter again supported 81st Infantry Division with nine Tigers of 1st and 2nd companies. Bölter's Tiger was knocked out, according to German sources, by a captured 8.8cm gun, on 13 August, killing the gunner and loader. The radio operator was killed by machine-gun fire while fleeing. Bölter escaped and survived the ordeal; supporting infantry in their armoured personnel carrier (APC) heard Bölter's distress call and found him.

# MEMEL, OCTOBER 1944

On 12 and 13 October 1944, the Germans attempted to throw Soviet infantry from hills near Memel with 20 tanks and two battalions of infantry from PGD *GD* and Tigers from 502nd Heavy Panzer Battalion. Two ISU-152s would be set on fire on Hill 32.3. By the end of 13 October, only five 336th *TSAP* ISU-152s would remain operational. The following day, the Soviets reported 20 Tigers with a battalion of infantry assaulting Hill 20.7 (this was probably a mix of vehicles, as the number of operational Tigers in the Memel perimeter was less); the German attack was beaten off, with one ISU-152 burnt. Soviet attacks on 20 October supported by a battery of ISU-152s could not breach Memel's defences. In October, 336th *TSAP* lost 26 killed, including five officers, and 28 wounded, among them nine officers. The commander would laud the inclusion of sappers to clear mines and ford water, and SMG soldiers to protect crews.

Also forming part of the attack on Memel was 376th *TSAP*, supporting 18th Tank Brigade of 5th GTA. The ISU-152s had moved 100km from Riga to Memel with 5th GTA on 29 September, and were initially attached to 3rd GTB. The attack began on 6 October. A German counter-attack was launched on 10 October. The 502nd Heavy Panzer Battalion with 13 Tigers from 1st and 2nd companies did not lose any Tigers in the attack. On 10 October, 3rd GTB captured Yakubovo with 18th Tank Brigade following.

In late September, the 336th *TSAP*, with 14 ISU-152s attached to 19th Rifle Corps, 43rd Army was tasked to support 344th Rifle Division in an attack against German defences near Memel, to begin on 5 October. The battalion commanders of 1152nd Rifle Regiment each had a battery of 336th *TSAP* and, with their battery commanders, studied the forward edge of enemy defences exposed by combat reconnaissance. Here, an ISU-152 moves forward accompanied by Soviet infantry. (Courtesy of the Central Museum of the Armed Forces, Moscow via Stavka)

The *GD* Tiger battalion was deployed to the Baltic States in August 1944, participating in the offensive to retake Siaulai between 18 and 25 August. The battalion was in the Memel defensive area from 10 October to 28 November. The Tigers had suffered from fuel shortages and many would be destroyed for lack of fuel in October prior to the PGD *GD* occupation of the Memel perimeter. The 1st and 2nd companies of 502nd Heavy Panzer Battalion were with them; 3rd Coy was in the Kurland pocket with 510th Heavy Panzer Battalion. The 1/502nd and 2/502nd would sail from Memel to Danzig in January 1945. The 3/502nd would give its six Tigers to 510th Heavy Panzer Battalion when it also embarked to Danzig. The morale of crews started to falter as losses mounted. (Nik Cornish at www.Stavka.org.uk)

Shishkin recalled combat with 18th Tank Brigade near Memel. The brigade had 20 T-34s in some woods with Shishkin's battery deployed in bushes on the edge of the wood. Beyond a field in front lay a hill with bushes on it. The brigade commander ordered the battalion commanders to advance on the hill. Before the attack was launched, Shishkin spotted some German armour to the left of the hill. He moved his SU-152s into firing positions and started to hit them at 1,000m range. Still, when the advance commenced, three T-34s were quickly knocked out and the rest pulled back to the wood. A company's worth was knocked out in three attacks. The battalion commander threatened to shoot the brigade commander if he ordered another attack. Shishkin was ordered to make a lateral march along the front. When an enemy reconnaissance aircraft noticed this, the pilot, according to Shishkin, must have radioed that the ISU-152s had departed. Shishkin received a signal to go back to their original position. The Germans had attacked. A major was identified and he told Shishkin that Tigers were approaching. Five or six T-34s were observed exiting the wood, all that remained in the brigade. When Shishkin reached his original position, he noticed five Tigers heading towards him 400m away. The battery's first salvo knocked out four; the fifth took cover behind a building. Shishkin ordered an ISU-152 to go along the ditch toward the building to knock it out. He was probably writing about the German attack on 10 October, though claiming Tigers destroyed when 502nd Heavy Panzer Battalion did not list any destroyed is inconsistent. In ten days, 18th Tank Brigade lost 22 tanks. 5th GTA was withdrawn on 13 October.

# NIKOLAI SHISHKIN

Nikolai Konstantinovich Shishkin was born in 1921 in Chelyabinsk. He enrolled in the Ural Polytechnic Institute in Sverdlovsk in 1939, then volunteered for military service when war was declared on Finland. He trained to be gun crew, deployed to the Karelian Isthmus, and participated in the assault on the Mannerheim Line. He was a junior sergeant and gun commander in 335th Rifle Regiment. By the end of the year he was part of the Leningrad garrison, and in September 1942 participated in operations to break the siege. In 1943 he was sent to artillery school in Saratov. In April, with the rank of lieutenant, he was appointed commander of an SU-152 in 1545th *SAP*. He participated in the Orel counter-offensive with 30th Tank Corps from 4th Tank Army. From the end of 1943 to the beginning of 1944, 1545th *SAP* was in training. In April 1944, Shishkin fought in the Targus Frumos area with 5th GTA; the formation was now 376th *TSAP* and he was a battery commander. From 2 to 5 May, his battery claimed three Tigers and two SP guns destroyed. Shishkin's SU-152 was the target of an enemy air sortie and a bomb splinter wounded him.

In October the regiment was ordered to entrain at Vainode station for Warsaw. In January 1945, 376th *TSAP* was ordered to advance into East Prussia. Shishkin's battery was astride the Elbing–Königsberg railway and stopped German forces from breaking out to the west. He was recommended for the title Hero of the Soviet Union, but instead was awarded the Order of the Red Banner.

Shishkin was sent to study at the Military Academy of Armoured Forces in May 1945. Upon completion of his post graduate studies, he worked at the Department of Tactics, later writing a doctoral thesis and being appointed professor. He taught operational art to many senior military officers from many different countries. He retired from the army in 1989 with the rank of colonel. In the 1990s he taught at the Military Academy of the General Staff of the Russian Federation Armed Forces. Shishkin passed away in 2010.

# UKRAINE, JULY–AUGUST 1944

On 6 June 1944, 1548th *SAP* was issued ISU-152s and renamed 349th *TSAP*, commanded by Guards Lieutenant Colonel N.P. Shishov, deploying to Konev's 1st Ukrainian Front. Batteries were attached to divisions of 101st Rifle Corps for the July offensive. Assault groups of two T-34s with two ISU-152s and four SU-76s were formed. The infantry attacked German defensive positions on 15 July. Elements of 1st and 8th Panzer divisions counter-attacked. Heavy artillery and aircraft were brought in to disrupt the German armour. Moving on roads, 8th Panzer Division was easily interdicted. The 3rd and 4th GTAs were introduced the next day in the area of 60th Army. German forces moved into the flank of the Soviet armour. On 15 July, 20–25 Tigers and Panthers, from 506th Heavy Panzer Battalion and 8th Panzer Division, attacked 349th *TSAP* while supporting 101st Rifle Corps, engaged in blocking encircled German positions at Brody. Six ISU-152s were lost, although the German attacks were unsuccessful. On 17 July, the remaining 13 operational ISU-152s were concentrated with 183rd Rifle Division. The 506th Heavy Panzer Battalion departed to be equipped with King Tigers, leaving its Tigers with 507th Heavy Panzer Battalion in Poland.

On the night of 12/13 August, 13 ISU-152s were surrounded in Ocekhov with only two platoons of SMG soldiers. German infantry used AT mines to destroy an ISU-152. Another three were heavily damaged. Gathering around Hill 458, the regiment was attacked during the day; two ISU-152s were hit and burned. The Germans lost four Pz IVs and some APCs in the engagement. By the evening, 349th *TSAP* broke out of

An ISU-152 with Soviet infantry on board. In December 1944, 349th *TSAP* operated with 33rd and 34th GRC of 5th Guards Army. In January 1945, four ISU-152s would support the attack of each assault battalion. Enemy fortifications were carefully studied and tactical exercises rehearsed. Shishov established three command posts for himself, the chief of staff and the deputy commander, to establish what was going on. By day two of the offensive, 349th *TSAP* claimed four Tigers burned, and four AT guns and eight bunkers destroyed. Shishov noted the use of individual ISU-152s in the open was not sensible, as the enemy targeted them with all weapons. In February, he ordered ISU-152 commanders to make their own decisions on the battlefield to best destroy targets. (From the fonds of the *RGAKFD* in Krasnogorsk via Stavka)

encirclement with an infantry company in support. Shishov spoke of the lack of infantry support for the ISUs, an absence of integral machine guns and the failure of 101st Rifle Corps guns to support them. Eight operational ISU-152s were then parcelled out among the rifle divisions of 101st Rifle Corps. The unit was soon withdrawn from the front, because most of the vehicles needed factory repair. A service life of 239 to 253 hours of engine time was the limit in the dusty summer heat. In August, 15 officers and sergeants were killed, 33 wounded and three ISU-152s burned.

## ROLE CHANGES

By late 1944, German crews would question whether having a smaller number of heavy tanks compared to a larger number of other vehicles was a good idea. Officers persisted in their belief in the Tiger. Senior officers wanted to use them to bolster the morale of the infantry close to the front, despite Tiger officers wanting to keep them concentrated further back to ease maintenance concerns. The importance of Tigers as symbols of military power would lead them to be shared out to support numerous operations. However, the Tiger's tactical achievements could not challenge the Allies' strategic superiority. They would be used to carry out missions not designed for them. The German leadership did not allocate them for the specific tasks in the environments for which they were originally built.

The economic realities of the German war economy by 1944 should have led to an expansion of Panther production and SP guns. Instead, Hitler, with Albert Speer's acquiescence, developed an even more expensive, heavier Tiger to show the Allies Germany was getting stronger, not weaker. A slow, deliberate defence was not chosen by the German command; it would instead persist with seeking tactical superiority. The presence of heavier Soviet armour justified to the proponents of the Tiger its continued development, to include the 8.8cm *KwK* 43 L/71. The new Tiger would be called Type B or King Tiger. Using a *Pzgr* 39-1 round, the shell could penetrate 148mm of armour from 1,500m. Using a *Pzgr* 40/43 round, the shell could penetrate 170mm of armour from the same distance. Five hundred King Tigers would be produced. The prototype was ready by December 1943. Speer, Minister of Armaments and War Production, directed that the Panther engine would be fitted into the King Tiger to simplify production and logistics. King Tiger production was scaled up to full capacity by June 1944. Tiger I production would end by August. Henschel was told to overlap the production of both to ensure no interruption of Tigers for the front. The Panther engine would not be powerful enough for the King Tiger.

The King Tiger's gun and thicker armour were capable of defeating the IS-2. By the end of 1944, opinions among crews started to change, because the Soviets could negate the Tiger's superiority through sheer numbers. When engaged frontally by heavy Soviet armour like the IS-2, the King Tigers would be outmanoeuvred by SP AT guns in a position to hit the King Tiger's side armour. The ISU-152 would not be needed in the AT role. Instead its use in cities would be optimized.

This is probably an ISU-152, though it looks like an SU-152, because sources state the image is on an East Prussian road in 1945. *TSAP* would often work with infantry during the fighting in Poland and Germany, using direct fire on enemy strong points. (From the fonds of the *RGAKFD* in Krasnogorsk via Stavka)

# ANALYSIS

While the success of Tigers in supporting infantry against hordes of Soviet armour was unarguable, the utility of Tigers to offensive operations was questionable, because they could not exploit breakthroughs they created due to maintenance and fuel issues. The presence of Tigers on the front also indicated where the point of main effort would be, and the Soviets developed multiple lines of defence with forward AT guns and mines in order to stop the Tiger intervening decisively. Tigers would be most effective in defence in small groups. Assigned to other formations, they would save the day by preventing enemy armour from exploiting a breach in the line. The inclusion of some Tigers in every Panzer division and Panzergrenadier division would have given these formations numerous offensive and defensive capabilities. The Tiger companies belonging to divisions were certainly worthwhile, achieving notable results. Supply problems would have occurred, limiting the tactical advantages this organization accrued. Adherence to the principle of concentration in defensive operations limited flexibility, and Tiger battalions would send companies and sometimes platoons to different sections of the front. Keeping battalions together did make sense from a logistical and maintenance point of view, because maintenance assets were lacking. However, to permit tactical flexibility, they needed to possess an equal travel range to the enemy formations they were expected to defeat. Tigers did not have this and thus needed to be deployed in smaller groupings. Defensive doctrine was limited and did not advise this approach. This occurred in the restricted terrain in Army Group North. Small groups could block avenues of approach. Deployed throughout the operational area, most Soviet breakthroughs could easily be reached prior to the defensive line collapsing. Such operations were helped by the incorporation of lighter armour. Offensive operations, though, would be hampered by lighter armour.

Germany was never going to equal the Allies' armour production. Committing the resources to the Tiger programme when they knew this was the case was a strategic error. Production of cheaper armour was probably the approach they should have used. The German leadership could not accept strategic reality. The German Army had no choice; it had to use these large offensively minded organizations on the defensive. Though initial success could be achieved when used to attack, by 1944 the German Army did not have the resources to exploit any success.

The SU-152 was never the nemesis of the Tiger that Soviet propaganda made it out to be. The encounters SU-152s had with Tigers were frequently because Tigers were being asked to support infantry formations that were being attacked by Soviet infantry armies that had SP gun support. In late 1943 and early 1944, Soviet armour, whether it was the independent tank regiments or the tank brigades, was being squandered and commanders only had SP guns to help stymie German counter-attacks. The use of SU-152s by the independent tank regiments was not by design. Frequently, by sheer luck, SU-152s would be given to tank regiments instead of KV-1S. The *SAP* would, for example, be pulled from the line to be equipped with ISU-152s and the SU-152s would be incorporated with heavy tank regiments. The SU-152, with its low rate of fire and limited on-board ammunition, was not an effective AT weapon. The ISU-152 did not change things substantially, though its better armour permitted it to stand against heavy German armour when needed, allowing the T-34/85s to work around the flanks. The IS-2 could perform this role, as could the ISU-122 with its better rate of fire. Ultimately, the ISU-152 would find its best utility in the urban environments of Germany.

The importance of ISU-152s to urban fighting was soon seen in 1945, and sometimes Tigers would be encountered. For example, 349th *TSAP* supported the Breslau assault in March by allocating batteries to infantry divisions. Heavy losses were experienced; however, most could be recovered. Breslau's defences had 47 tanks including 20 Tigers or Panthers, firing from behind barricades. Losses to the ISU-152s were low, despite the dense AT fortifications in the city. Thorough reconnaissance determined where enemy guns were positioned. Thirty rounds were carried in the ISU-152 and trucks had another 25 per vehicle nearby. (From the fonds of the *RGAKFD* in Krasnogorsk via Stavka)

# BIBLIOGRAPHY

Anderson, T., *Tiger*, Osprey Publishing Ltd., Oxford, 2017

Biryuk, S., *Bitva za Pskov: Aprel 1944*, Yauza, Moscow, 2019

Carius, O., *Tigers in the Mud*, Stackpole Books, Mechanicsburg, PA, 2003

Doyle, H. and Jentz, T., *Tiger 1 Heavy Tank 1942–45*, Osprey Publishing Ltd., Oxford, 1993

Drabkin, A., *Panzer Killers*, Pen and Sword, Barnsley, 2013

Kurowski, F., *Panzer Aces*, Stackpole Books, Mechanicsburg, PA, 2004

Pasholok, Y., *The SU-152*, Lombardy Studios, Oakland, CA, 2020

Pudovkin, S.I., *Uralskiye Zveroboi potiv nemetskogo Zverintsa*, Nizhny Tagil, 2020

Schneider, W., *Tigers in Combat I*, J.J. Fedorowicz, Winnipeg, Manitoba, 1998

Schneider, W., *Tigers in Combat II*, J.J. Fedorowicz, Winnipeg, Manitoba, 2000

Wilbeck, C.W., *Sledgehammers: The Strengths and Flaws of Tiger Tank Battalions in World War II*, Aberjona Press, Bedford, PA, 2004

An ISU-152 tank preserved at Kubinka Tank Museum, Russia. The museum is located about an hour's drive from Moscow. (Ieee5392, CC BY-SA 4.0)

# ACRONYMS

| | |
|---|---|
| APC | armoured personnel carrier |
| APCBC | Armour Piercing Cap Ballistic Cap |
| AT | anti-tank |
| GA | Guards Army |
| *GABTU* | Main Automotive Armoured Tank Directorate |
| *GAU* | Main Artillery Directorate |
| GCC | Guards Cavalry Corps |
| *GD* | *Grossdeutschland* |
| GHTR | Guards Heavy Tank Regiment |
| *GKO* | State Defence Committee |
| GMB | Guards Motorcycle Battalion |
| GMC | Guards Mechanized Corps |
| GR | Grenadier Regiment |
| GTA | Guards Tank Army |
| GTB | Guards Tank Battalion |
| GTC | Guards Tank Corps |
| HMG | heavy machine gun |
| MB | mechanized brigade |
| MC | mechanized corps |
| MRB | motorized rifle brigade |
| PC | Panzer corps |
| PD | Panzer division |
| PGD *GD* | Panzergrenadier Division *Grossdeutschland* |
| Pz | Panzer |
| RC | rifle corps |
| RD | rifle division |
| *RGAKFD* | Russian State Documentary Film and Photo Archive |
| RR | rifle regiment |
| *SAP* | self-propelled artillery regiment |
| SMG | sub-machine gun |
| SPG | self-propelled gun |
| TA | tank army |
| TB | tank brigade |
| TC | tank corps |
| TR | tank regiment |
| *TSAP* | heavy self-propelled artillery regiment |
| *TZF* | *TurmZielFernrohr* (turret sighting telescope) |
| *UZTM* | Ural Heavy Machinery Plant |

# INDEX